INTERMEDIATE ENGLISH LANGUAGE SKILLS

Mary M Firth
Andrew G Ralston

Illustrations by

O. R. Davison and M. E. Ralston

SCOTTISH EXAMINATION MATERIALS

HODDER GIBSON

INTRODUCTION

This book is designed as a preparation for Intermediate English examinations. It aims to provide hints in what is known as 'exam technique' in order that students understand exactly what is wanted in examination questions and can thus achieve the best possible result.

Frequent checklists are included to help the student focus on the aspects of language which the different types of question require.

Simple step by step explanations are followed by practice exercises which aim to teach the skills required to answer the more formal type of questions in both Close Reading and Textual Analysis. Sample tests of both types of exercise are provided to help students prepare for the examinations more directly.

MMF / AGR

Orders: please contact Bookpoint Ltd, 130 Milton Park, Abingdon, Oxon OX14 4SB. Telephone: (44) 01235 827720. Fax: (44) 01235 400454. Lines are open from 9.00–6.00, Monday to Saturday, with a 24 hour message answering service. You can also order through our website www.hoddereducation.co.uk.

British Library Cataloguing in Publication Data
A catalogue record for this title is available from the British Library

ISBN-13: 978-0-716-96018-8

Published by Hodder Gibson, 2a Christie Street, Paisley PA1 1NB.
Tel: 0141 848 1609; Fax: 0141 889 6315; email: hoddergibson@hodder.co.uk
First Published 2001
Impression number   10 9
Year   2011

Copyright © 2001 Firth & Ralston

Cover photo © Steve Prezant/CORBIS
Printed in Great Britain for Hodder Gibson, an imprint of Hodder Education, an Hachette UK Company, 2a Christie Street, Paisley, PA1 1NB, Scotland, UK by MPG Books, Bodmin

CONTENTS

PART ONE: CLOSE READING SKILLS

PART ONE:

CLOSE READING SKILLS

CLOSE READING

In Intermediate English, the Close Reading part of the course aims to test fully your understanding of language. The text will be prose and it will be a piece of non-fiction, such as a newspaper article.

The questions on the text will focus on **three** aspects of it:

> **What** the writer is saying (**Understanding**);
> **How** the writer is saying it (**Analysis**);
> **How effectively** he is saying it (**Evaluation**).

In the exam, you will see the letters **U**, **A** or **E** after each question. (Occasionally a question will test a combination of these.) This is to help you know what kind of answer is wanted.

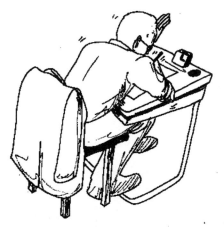

Exam Technique

The art of answering test questions in the correct way is called **'exam technique'**. Often, marks are lost not through lack of real understanding, but through a failure to grasp exactly what is wanted by the examiners in certain types of question.

The following pages contain hints in answering the three types of question in the way that examiners expect. There are also exercises for practice.

Directed questions

The questions in the texts of Close Reading in Intermediate English are always 'directed'. This means you will be told to look at a particular section of the text to find the answers. For example, you will be given pointers such as 'in the first paragraph' or 'Look at lines . . .'

It is very important that you follow these instructions carefully. It can be helpful to mark off the directed section in some way - with brackets, underlining or by means of a highlighter pen.

Direction to a section of text is helpful as it saves time searching through the whole of it.

However, you *must* be sure to supply an answer from within the section you are directed to. If you choose an answer from outside the section you will get no marks.

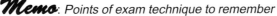

Memo: *Points of exam technique to remember*

Find the answer **within the lines you are directed to** in the text.

Note the **number of marks** available and give an answer of a suitable length and amount of detail.

Look carefully at what the question instructs you to do. **Use your own words** unless the answer asks you to **quote**.

Note carefully what type of answer is required: **understanding** (what is said), **analysis** (how it is said) or **evaluation** (how effectively it is said) .

UNDERSTANDING

Some questions will be set to test your **understanding** of a text.

1. Factual Questions

The most common task is to be asked to pick out a fact from the text and express it in your own words.

Here is an example from the 2000 Intermediate 2 paper. The topic of this text was 'a notorious species of spider', the tarantula, and the narrator was the spider itself.

> I'm nocturnal. I love the moonlight, the shadows, the dark places, the dappled murk. I'm not being poetic. I'm simply being true to my nature, my nocturnal nature. Like all tarantulas.
>
> Question: **In your own words**, in what way is the speaker 'like all tarantulas' according to the first paragraph? (1 Mark)

There are two steps to answering a question of this type.

Step One:
Look in the text for the information which will answer the question. In this case, it is provided by the word 'nocturnal'.

Step Two:
Express the information **in your own words** in a simple sentence which fits the way the question is worded. In this example you had to change from 1st person ('I') into 3rd person ('the speaker').

An acceptable answer to gain the mark would be :

The speaker is active by night.

Remember, if you were simply to say 'The speaker is nocturnal' or 'He is nocturnal' you would get no marks since you would have failed to do step two, namely to **use your own words**.

You may put the original word or words from the text in brackets after your own version. This will make it quite clear to the examiner that you have focused on the right part of the text. Your answer would thus read:

> The speaker is active by night
> (nocturnal).

Remember that such additions, while helpful to the examiner, will cost you time and so should be kept to a minimum.

A variation of this task is a question which asks you to pick out *a number of points* the writer makes and repeat them briefly in your own words. Such a question frequently includes the word '**summarise**'. Here is an example from the 2000 Intermediate 2 paper:

> *The speaker provides several pieces of evidence to support his argument that the fear of tarantulas is unjustified.*
>
> *Summarise the main ones given in lines 88–113. (3 marks)*

In this question, the number of marks available, three, suggests the number of pieces of evidence to be found. Always remember to look **carefully** at the number of marks. A summary question may be worth as many as 5 marks, and you must try to persuade the examiner to give you all of these. You might choose to present your answer in a numbered format.

1. . . .
2. . . .
3. . . .

This will help gain you a mark for each separate point made.

Warning! One of the commonest errors of exam technique is to write too *much* for a single mark question, and too *little* for a multiple mark question.

For Practice

Answer the questions attached to the following pieces of text. Go through the two steps outlined above for each question. Check carefully the number of marks available. In the first two examples, step one is done for you and the part of the text which provides the answer is underlined, so that you need only concentrate on expressing the ideas in your own words.

1. Stories about haunted places are always fascinating. What goes on there, and how, and why? Some hauntings can be explained as the results of ordinary trickery. In others some natural cause is at work, though it has not yet been traced.

    (Aidan Chambers *Book of Ghosts and Hauntings* © 1973)

    Question:

    *What **two** explanations does the writer suggest to account for the belief that some places are haunted? (2 marks)*

2. Harrison started out as a carpenter. He completed his first pendulum clock in 1713, before he was twenty years old. Why he came to take on this project and how he excelled at it with no experience as a watchmaker's apprentice remain mysteries. Aside from the fact that the great John Harrison built it, the clock claims uniqueness for another feature: it is constructed almost entirely of wood. Harrison, ever practical and resourceful, took what materials came to hand and handled them well. This is a carpenter's clock.

    (Dava Sobel *Longitude* © 1995)

    Questions:

    (a) *What are the **two** 'mysteries' which puzzle the writer concerning the building of John Harrison's first clock? (2 marks)*

    (b) *What is unusual about the construction of the clock, and why did Harrison choose this form of construction? (2 marks)*

3. Smugglers used to spread rumours that the places where they landed their cargoes were haunted. This made local people keep away, and accounted for strange lights seen flitting about after dark, or peculiar

sounds. Today just occasionally tenants who want to be moved from one house to another have been known to stage a 'haunt'.

(Aidan Chambers *Book of Ghosts and Hauntings* © 1973)

Question:

*What **two** reasons does the writer give for smugglers pretending that their landing places were haunted? (2 marks)*

4. The benefits of liking football at school were simply incalculable. I was the only Arsenal supporter in first year. But in that glorious first football-saturated term, it didn't matter that I was on my own. In any case, my new best friend, a Derby County fan, was similarly isolated. The main thing was that you were a believer.

    Transferring to secondary school was easy. I was probably the smallest boy in the first year, but my size didn't matter, although my friendship with the Derby fan, the tallest by several feet, was pretty handy; and though my performance as a student was undistinguished (I was bunged into the 'B' stream at the end of the year and stayed there throughout my entire grammar school career), the lessons were a breeze. Even the fact that I was one of only three boys wearing shorts wasn't as traumatic as it should have been. As long as you knew the name of the Burnley manager nobody much cared that you were an eleven-year-old dressed as a six-year-old.

(Nick Hornby *Fever Pitch* © 1992)

Question:

*The writer states that his interest in football helped him fit in to his new school and get on with his schoolmates. What **three** facts does he mention that might have made things difficult for him? (3 marks)*

5.   My childhood was a not altogether happy one. Circumstances conspired to make me shy and solitary. My father and mother died before I was capable of remembering them. I was an only child, entrusted to the care of an unmarried aunt who lived quietly in the country. My aunt was no longer young when I began to live in her comfortable old-fashioned house with its large, untidy garden. She had settled down to her local interests, seldom had anyone to stay with her and rarely left home. She was fond of her two Persian cats, busied herself with the garden and was charitably interested in the old inhabitants of the village. Beyond this, the radius of her activities extended no further than eight or ten miles.

(Siegfried Sassoon *Memoirs of a Foxhunting Man*)

Question:

The author gives several reasons for his childhood being 'not altogether happy'.

(a) Summarise the main ones. (4 marks)

*(b) Suggest **one** thing he mentions that might have cheered him up, and explain why you think it might have done so. (2 marks)*

2. Meanings of Words

Another task set to test understanding is to explain the meaning of a word or phrase used in the text. Sometimes you will be asked to pick out a clue near to the word or phrase in the text which makes this meaning clear. The word **context** may be used here. The context means the part of the text where the word is used.

Look again at the opening paragraph of the text on the tarantula:

I'm nocturnal. I love the moonlight, the shadows, the dark places, the dappled murk. I'm not being poetic. I'm simply being true to my nature, my nocturnal nature. Like all tarantulas.

Consider this question :

Show how the context helps you understand the meaning of 'nocturnal'.
(2 marks)

Again there are two steps to answering this type of question.

Step one:

Explain the meaning of the word.

Step two:

Show how the rest of the text makes this clear by **quoting** the word or words which provide clues.

An acceptable answer might be:

> 'Nocturnal' means being active by night. The writer refers to his preference for 'moonlight' and 'dark' which both suggest night-time.

For Practice

Show how the context helps you understand the meaning of the words printed in italics in the following pieces of text. Remember that you must first give the meaning, and then show what clues help you to reach this. Each question is worth 2 marks.

1. 1968 was, I suppose, the most *traumatic* year of my life. After my parents' separation we moved into a smaller house, but for a time, because of some sort of chain, we were homeless and had to stay with our neighbours; I became seriously ill with jaundice; and I started at the local grammar school.

    (Nick Hornby *Fever Pitch* © 1972)

2. Saturday afternoon is a festive day with the natives. The girls put on all the *finery* they can on Saturday afternoon — silk robes, hats trimmed with fresh flowers and home-made necklaces of vermilion tinted blossoms.

    (Mark Twain *Roughing it in the Sandwich Islands*)

3. There are many ordinary happenings which have frightened or startled people into believing they were caused by ghostly means. *Subterranean* movements of earth and rock in old mine-workings, for instance, can cause very odd noises, and miners hearing tappings and rumblings in the underground darkness used to be sure they were made either by earth spirits or by the spirits of other miners long dead.

    (Aidan Chambers *Book of Ghosts and Hauntings* © 1973)

4. Presently we came to a place where no grass grew — a wide expanse of deep sand. All around everywhere, not three feet apart, the bleached bones of men gleamed white in the moonlight. Nothing whatever is known about this place — its story is a secret that will never be revealed. The oldest natives make no pretence of knowing its history. They say the bones were here when their grandfathers were children — but how they came here they can only _conjecture_. Many people believe this spot to be an ancient battle-ground, and it is usual to call it so.

(Extract from Mark Twain _Roughing it in the Sandwich Islands_)

5. I was born at Blunderstone in Suffolk. I was a _posthumous_ child. My father's eyes had closed upon the light of this world six months when mine opened on it. There is something strange to me even now, in the reflection that he never saw me; and something stranger yet in the shadowy remembrance that I have of my first childish associations with his white gravestone in the churchyard.

(Charles Dickens _David Copperfield_)

6. About this time my brother's behaviour grew ever more _unpredictable_. On a good day he would be cheerful and behave almost like the Matthew of old. A bad day might see him do anything from sinking into a silent depression to throwing the furniture in his room.

7. For me, a detention was in fact a thoroughly _congenial_ hour. I could lose myself in the drama of my history books and surrender to my imagination in the production of an English composition. But most of all, I was for the duration safe and secure from the taunts of Ranzio and his gang.

8. If it had not been for a _benevolent_ old lady, Oliver would most certainly have fallen dead on the highway. But the old lady, who had a grandson wandering in some distant part of the world, took pity on Oliver, and gave him what little she could afford and more, and with kind and gentle words.

ANALYSIS

Analysis questions ask you to think about **how** the writer is expressing his ideas. A common fault of exam technique is to treat an analysis question as if it is one of understanding. Marks are often lost in these questions because candidates explain **what** is being said rather than **how** it is said. Remember that analysis questions will be marked with an 'A' to jog your memory about this.

Analysis questions will deal with aspects of style: sentence structure and punctuation; expression and word choice; figures of speech; the structure of the argument; and tone.

Look very carefully at the wording of the question to find out what is wanted. If the question asks you to '**Quote**', you may simply pick out a word or expression from the text. Such questions are usually worth only 1 mark.

Here is an example from a past paper of such a question :

Quote the expression that makes it clear . . .

However, more usually an answer to an Analysis question will require you to explain something in your own words.

Almost always you will be expected to quote something *as well as* providing an explanation in your own words. A question on word choice will *always* require both quotation and explanation. Here is a typical example of a question which requires you both to quote and comment:

> Select one expression used to describe this and explain why you find it effective.

1. Sentence Structure

The most important thing is to know what is meant by sentence structure, and what an answer on it should refer to. You should not only **describe the main features** of sentence structure but also **explain their effect**.

Basically, the 'structure of a sentence' means the way in which it is made up, and how the various elements are arranged. The punctuation can be helpful in giving clues to the structure.

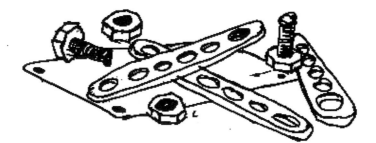

Step One:

Look out for the types of sentence the writer uses.

Here are the main types and the *effect* each type is likely to have:

Memo:

♦ **Statements** — tell you something. They end in a full stop. Most sentences are statements, so it is usually if *other* types of sentence are used that you will need to comment. Writing which is made up of statements alone may have a calm or impersonal tone.

♦ **Questions** — ask something. They *always* end with a question mark. Using questions may challenge the reader, or show uncertainty in the writer. Look out for **rhetorical questions**, which do not expect an answer, e.g., 'What kind of an answer is that?' Such questions aim to stir up strong feelings in the reader, such as anger. They create what is called an *emotive* tone, which simply means one which stirs up feelings or emotions.

♦ **Commands** — tell you to *do* something. 'Think of a number'. They end with either a full stop or an exclamation mark. They are often used in advertisements or where the writer tries to create the effect of talking directly to the reader.

♦ **Exclamations** — express excitement or surprise. 'How beautiful it was!' 'What a place!' 'Goodness gracious!' Exclamations do not always contain verbs. They often begin with 'What' or 'How', like the first two examples, and end in either an exclamation mark or a full stop. Exclamations may also create an *emotive* or *dramatic* tone.

♦ **Minor Sentences** — don't contain a verb. Since they are abbreviations of other types of sentence they may end in a full stop or a question mark. 'What now?' 'Time for a rest'. Such sentences will be very short and may create a tense or dramatic mood. They are typical of informal language and may be used in direct speech, notes or diary entries. Such writing without verbs may also be called **note form**.

For Practice

Say whether each of these sentences is a statement, a command, a question, an exclamation or a minor sentence.

1. What time does the match start?

2. Give me the money.

3. What an ordeal my interview turned out to be!

4. What do people care nowadays?

5. The dance will begin at nine o'clock.

6. Eleven thirty. Still no sign of anyone!

7. Why is she so upset?

8. Come in!

9. Quite right!

10. He came here many years ago.

♦ This exercise is just for practice in recognising the different sentence types. You will never be asked simply to *identify* types of sentence; you will always be asked to explain the *effect* of choosing particular types. This is only possible when you know the full context.

Step Two:

Consider whether sentences are long and complex or short and simple.

Long sentences containing several verbs and therefore several clauses are called **complex**. These are typical of written English, and usually, the more complex the sentences, the more formal the language.

e.g., *It is merely to suspect that physicians marry quality with quantity when they judge how far to intervene.*

Sentences with only one verb are called **simple**. These are typical of speech and types of language which aim to communicate very quickly and directly. Young children, for example, tend to use mainly simple sentences.

e.g., *The older generation are a canny bunch.*

Step Three:

Look at the arrangement of words within the sentence, particularly in longer ones. Some of the following features may be worth commenting on.

Word Order

The best advice is that anything unusual probably deserves a comment. A reversal of the normal word order is known as **inversion**, e.g., 'back we went' instead of 'we went back'. Using inversion throws emphasis on to a particular part of the sentence — in this example it is the word 'back' which is stressed.

Particular Patterns in Sentences

Often a pattern will be clear to see in a sentence.

Three patterns are specially common: **list**
repetition
climax

Julius Caesar's legendary saying 'I came, I saw, I conquered' is an example of all three of these techniques at once.

The **list** of verbs 'came, saw and conquered' creates a sense of action.

The **repetition** of the personal pronoun 'I' suggests a speaker who is egotistical and dominating.

The verbs in the list have a sense of progress and end with the most powerful, leading to the effect of a **climax**.

Parts of Speech

The words which make up a sentence are called **parts of speech**. There are eight parts of speech in English, which all have different functions: **nouns**, **verbs**, **adjectives**, **adverbs**, **pronouns**, **prepositions**, **conjunctions** and **articles**. It is useful to be able to identify these so that you can comment if any part of speech is used in an unusual way to create a particular effect.

Conjunctions, which have a linking function, are often worthy of comment. In the case of verbs, recognising the **tense** can be useful. In most narrative writing the **past** tense is used. If the **present** tense is used, or if the tense changes at some point, this may well be worth commenting on.

◆ Be precise in describing the effects. You will get little credit for vague comments such as 'the writer uses a lot of adjectives'.

For Practice

Can you identify all the parts of speech underlined in this extract? There are two examples of each type.

> Scrooge recoiled in <u>terror</u>, <u>for</u> the scene had changed. <u>Now</u> <u>he</u> almost <u>touched</u> a bed, on which, <u>beneath</u> a <u>ragged</u> sheet, there lay a something covered up. The room was very dark. A <u>pale</u> light <u>fell</u> straight <u>upon</u> the bed, <u>and</u> on <u>it</u>, unwatched, unwept, uncared for, was <u>the</u> body of <u>a</u> man. The cover was so <u>carelessly</u> adjusted that the slightest raising of it, the motion of a <u>finger</u> on Scrooge's part, would have disclosed the face.

◆ Discuss:

What is the effect of the list of adjectives beginning with 'un-' in lines 4–5 of this extract?

Parenthesis

A **parenthesis** is an extra piece of information inserted into a sentence and enclosed by a pair of commas, brackets or dashes. The plural of this word is **parentheses**.

A parenthesis may be a single word, a phrase or a whole clause. While the grammar and basic sense of the sentence would remain intact if the parenthesis were omitted, it will add something significant. It may make the meaning clearer, by adding an explanation or clarifying detail:

> e.g., 'A girl, not of her set, called Judith, giggled.'

In this example from *The Prime of Miss Jean Brodie*, the first parenthesis implies a reason why the girl was impertinent enough to giggle, while the second makes clear which girl it was.

Alternatively, a parenthesis may affect the tone by adding a comment, which might be humorous or ironic; for example:

> 'On the friendly Greek island of Cephalonia, the Elephtherious (try saying that with a mouthful of moussaka) will welcome you with open arms.'

> 'The responsibility of the officer is to look after, to supervise, to lead (whatever that means).'

For Practice

Look at the passage on page 28. Pick out **two** examples of parenthesis and explain what each adds to the text.

First or Third Person

Does the text use pronouns such as I, me and we — **first person**? Or does it use he, she and they — **third person**? Although this may not be considered strictly a matter of structure, you will often be given credit for making a comment on the choice of 'person' a writer makes.

Punctuation

Punctuation is very useful in making clear the sentence structure. It would be worth learning this list of punctuation marks and their uses.

Memo:

Commas (,) separate phrases and clauses within a sentence. A number of commas may well indicate a **list**.

A **colon** (:) introduces a quotation or a list; an explanation or elaboration; or a summing up. There will often be a balance between the two parts of the sentence it divides.

A **semi-colon** (;) finishes off one part of a sentence. It may be used instead of a conjunction to separate two principal clauses in a sentence.

Inverted commas (' ') (" ")mark quotations, direct speech, foreign words or words used in an unusual way. (Italics may sometimes be used similarly.)

A **dash** (—) can function like a colon to introduce a quotation, list, explanation, elaboration or summing up; two dashes can mark off a parenthesis. (In typography, a dash is longer than a hyphen.)

A **hyphen** (-) joins two words to make a compound word, or indicates a split word at the end of a line.

For Practice

The following examples all focus on sentence structure and / or punctuation. The number of marks indicates how much you should write for each answer.

1. *(The narrator in this extract is a young boy who has lost his horse, Rob Roy.)*

    It would take me years to live down the disgrace. In the meantime I must hurry home as fast as my dismounted legs could carry me. If only I could catch sight of that wretched Rob Roy eating some more grass by the roadside! If only I hadn't let him go! If only I could begin my ride all over again! How careful I would be!

    Question:

    Show how the author uses sentence structure to emphasise the narrator's sense of shame and panic at losing his horse. (2 marks)

2. Scrooge became as good a friend, as good a master, and as good a man as the good old City knew.

    Question:

    How does Dickens use sentence structure to emphasise the dramatic way in which his character, Scrooge, has reformed? (2 marks)

3. We went on the ghost train; we went on the chairoplanes and we went on the waltzers; we went on the giant roller coaster; we even — plucking up our courage! — went on the rocket launcher that actually *turned upside down*; finally, heads spinning and stomachs heaving, we tottered down to the low wall at the sea front for a welcome gulp of fresh air.

    Question:

    *Show how the writer uses **two** features of sentence structure to emphasise the number of fairground rides the children went on, and how these get more and more daring. (2 marks)*

4. Of all bad deeds that, under cover of the darkness, had been committed within wide London's bounds since night hung over it, that was the worst. Of all the horrors that rose with an ill scent upon the morning air, that was the foulest and most cruel.

    Question:

    This comment is made about Bill Sykes's murder of Nancy in Dickens's 'Oliver Twist'. How does Dickens use sentence structure to emphasise the dramatic nature of the deed? (2 marks)

5. Here was room for the imagination to work! You could imagine those lights the width of a continent away — and that hidden under the intervening darkness were hills, and winding rivers, and weary wastes of plain and desert — and even then the tremendous vista stretched on, and on, and on! — to the fires and far beyond!

    Question:

    Show how the writer uses sentence structure to emphasise the huge extent of the crater of this giant volcano. (Look for sentence types, use of conjunctions and repetition. Use the punctuation as a clue.) (5 marks)

6. "Er, excuse me. Excuse me. Excuse me, do you mind? Excuse me would you mind keeping it down just a little? Excu . . . look, are you just gonna SHUT UP !!??!!" About nine times out of ten, this is exactly the sort of thing you never say to the person behind you in the cinema.

Question:

Show how the writer uses sentence structure and punctuation to create a convincing picture of someone in a cinema plucking up the courage to complain to someone who is disturbing him by talking. (5 marks)

7. You couldn't see far and you couldn't see plain, but there was the deep sea moving on its way about the night earth, flat and quiet, the colour of grey mud, and here were the two of us alone in the high tower, and there, far out at first, was a ripple, followed by a wave, a rising, a bubble, a bit of froth. And then, from the surface of the cold sea came a head, a large head, dark-coloured, with immense eyes, and then a neck. And then — not a body — but more neck and more! Only then did the body, like a little island of black coral and shells and crayfish, drip up from the subterranean.

Question:

How does the writer use sentence structure to emphasise the immense size of the sea monster? (4 marks)

8. I well remember though, how the distant idea of the holidays, after seeming for an immense time to be a stationary speck, began to come towards us, and to grow and grow. How, from counting months, we came to weeks, and then to days; and how I then began to be afraid that I should not be sent for and, when I learnt from Steerforth that I had been sent for and was certainly to go home, had dim forebodings that I might break my leg first. How the breaking-up day changed its place fast, at last, from the week after next to next week, this week, the day after tomorrow, tomorrow, today, tonight — when I was inside the Yarmouth mail-coach, and going home.

Question:

Show how the writer uses sentence structure to show how time appears distorted to a small boy at boarding school who is desperate for the holidays to arrive. (4 marks)

9. At unequal distances all around the shores of the lake were nearly white-hot chimneys or hollow drums of lava, four or five feet high, and up through them were bursting gorgeous sprays of lava gouts and gem spangles, some white, some red and some golden — a ceaseless bombardment, and one that fascinated the eye with its unapproachable splendour.

Question:

Show how the author uses sentence structure to create a sense of drama in this description of a volcano erupting. (Points to note: the length of the sentence; the use of inversion in lines 2–3; the effects of repetition of certain phrases; and the relationship of the part of the sentence after the dash to the first part of description.) (5 marks)

10. Boldwood had turned quickly, taken one of the guns and at once fired it at Troy. Troy fell. The distance apart of the two men was so small that the charge of shot did not spread in the least, but passed like a bullet into his body. He uttered a long guttural sigh — there was a contraction — an extension — then his muscles relaxed, and he lay still.

Question:

Show how the author's sentence structure indicates the suddenness of the shooting and also presents the last moments of the victim realistically. (4 marks)

2. Expression and word choice

Questions relating to expression and word choice look at the effect created by the particular choices of the writer. The writer's tone will depend on these choices. The particular style a writer chooses is known as the **register**. This includes grammar, word choice and all aspects of style.

Colloquial language

A writer may choose to write **informally** using a style more typical of speaking than writing. This is called **colloquial** language. Expressions such as 'well', 'by the way', 'of course' and 'you know' are examples, as are slang words such as 'guy' for man or 'kid' for child.

The first question in the 2000 Intermediate paper focused on this aspect of expression.

> Quoting evidence from the early part of the passage (lines 1–20), show how the writer creates the impression of someone **speaking to us** rather than writing for us. (2 marks)

In this example, you were directed to quite a large section of the text, but as the question was worth only two marks you had to be selective. Here is a possible answer.

> The writer uses the word 'you' (in 'I guess you can tell') which gives the impression he is chatting to the reader. He also uses slang expressions such as 'guy' and 'in case you don't know' which add to the impression he is speaking.

For Practice

Read this article on the artist Vincent van Gogh.

Think of poor old Vincent and you think of . . . Kirk Douglas[1]? Philistine[2]!
You could talk about Vince at breakfast, dinner and tea for months, so
let's begin by scotching that old chestnut about his right ear. He didn't cut
it off, OK? Only the lobe. Meet Vincent van Gogh (1853–90), the eldest of
5 six children. He's stubborn and volatile[3], doesn't get on with his Dutch
pastor father, or his mother, and leaves home as soon as possible. His
brother Theo tries to find him a job. Alas. One hard-luck story leads to
another. Awkward young Vincent is unemployable as a picture dealer,
and as a teacher, and he hits the pits (sorry) as a lay preacher in the
10 Belgian coal-fields. Aged 27, he decides to become an artist and (at
Antwerp Academy) proves to be unteachable too. He learns what he can,
when he can, by bumming around. To judge by some of his terrific
drawings up to 1885, he learns a lot. Then, in 1886, he arrives on Theo's
doorstep in Paris. Theo has a family, but adds Vincent's money worries to
15 his own. Vincent's painting style changes completely. Before Paris, it's a
kind of atmospheric sludge. Once there, bright, vibrant colours are soon
in evidence, in a style influenced by a new love, Japanese prints. But
Vincent's drinking and bad temper haven't lessened, and in 1888 Theo's
relieved when Big Brother moves down south, to Arles.

(*ART A Crash Course* © The Ivy Press Limited, 1998)

[1]Kirk Douglas: actor who played van Gogh in a Hollywood film.
[2]Philistine: a person who knows nothing about art or culture.
[3]Volatile: moody.

This article is full of informal, colloquial features. Find two or more examples of each of the following and fill them in to the table. One or two are filled in to help you.

'Command' type of sentence structure	1. Think of. . . .(line 1) 2.
Sentences without verbs / lapses of written grammar rules	1. Philistine! (line 1) 2.
Informal expressions	1. that old chestnut (line 3) 2. 3. 4.
Use of second person (you)	1. You think of . . . (line 1) 2.
Informal reference to a person (e.g., use of first name or nickname)	1. poor old Vincent (line 1) 2. 3.
Abbreviations	1. let's begin (line 3) 2. 3.
Slang words or expressions	1.OK (line 4) 2. 3.

Dialect

One particular form of spoken English is **dialect**. Dialect is the name given to the style of language spoken in a particular area of the English speaking world. Scots is an example of a dialect. You may be asked to compare dialect with **Standard English**, which is the term you should use for the style of English that is understood everywhere. Dialect forms may be simply Standard English words pronounced differently, such as Scots 'auld' for 'old', or they may take the form of completely different words such as 'bairn' or 'wean' for 'child'.

Many Scots writers prefer using their own dialect to Standard English as they feel it is more natural, expressive and lively.

For Practice

In this poem, the writer, Liz Lochhead, adopts the persona of a child starting school who is forced to give up her own dialect and speak Standard English.

KIDSPOEM / BAIRNSANG

It wis January
and a gey dreich day
the first day I went to the school
so
5 ma Mum happed me up in ma good navyblue nap coat
wi the rid tartan hood
birled a scarf aroon ma neck
pu'ed on ma pixie and ma pawkies
it wis that bitter
10 said
'noo ye'll no starve'
gied me a wee kiss and a kidoan skelp on the bum
and sent me off across the playground
to the place I'd learn to say
15 'It was January
and a really dismal day
the first day I went to school
so
my Mother wrapped me up in my best navyblue top coat
20 with the red tartan hood
twirled a scarf around my neck
pulled on my bobble-hat and mittens
it was so bitterly cold
said

25 "now you won't freeze to death"
gave me a little kiss and a pretend slap on the bottom
and sent me off across the playground
to the place I'd learn to forget to say
"It wis January
30 and a gey dreich day
the first day I went to the school
so
ma Mum happed me up in ma good navyblue nap coat
wi the rid tartan hood
35 birled a scarf aroon ma neck
pu'ed on ma pixie and ma pawkies
it wis that bitter." '

Oh,
saying it was one thing
40 but when it came to writing it
in black and white
the way it had to be said
was as if
you were grown up, posh, male, English and dead.

© Liz Lochhead

Compare the sections that are in Scots and English.

Write down in two columns the words that are completely different. The first pair are entered for you.

Scots	*Standard English*
gey	really

Now add two or three examples of words which are given a different pronunciation in Scots. Try reading the poem aloud. Discuss how far you feel the Scots dialect is more effective than the Standard English version of the lines.

Shades of Meaning

Sometimes you may be asked to explain a particular shade of meaning of a word.

Look at this example from the 2000 Intermediate 2 paper :

> *Quote an expression from the first three paragraphs that suggests that the speaker does not feel threatened in the film theatre. (1 mark)*

The answer was 'saunter' (from 'I saunter in under the Ladies' Room door . . . ') which means to walk in a carefree manner. Since this question was worth only 1 mark and instructs you to 'quote', this one word was all that was required. There was no need to waste time on further explanation.

However, the question might have been set in the following way:

> *What does the word 'saunter' suggest about how the speaker feels in the theatre? (2 marks)*

If the question had been set in this way, an explanation **in your own words** would have been required. A good approach would be to consider what would have been lost if a more neutral word such as 'walk' had been used instead.

An acceptable answer would be:

> 'Saunter', meaning to walk in a carefree way, shows the speaker did not feel threatened in the movie theatre at all.

For Practice

Answer the following questions on **shades of meaning**. You may use a dictionary to help you with your answers.

1. (*The writer, a ten year old boy, has been allowed out riding alone for the first time. He dismounted to let the horse eat some grass and it had run away.*)

    I could have burst into tears at that moment but I managed to control my feelings. Half an hour afterwards I slunk into the stable yard with a sinking heart. No one seemed to be about.

    Question:

    Quote *the word which suggests the writer is so embarrassed he does not wish to be seen. (1 mark)*

2. (*The writer is returning to the trenches at night after a spell on leave during the first world war.*)

    Pushing past the gas-blanket, I blundered down the stairs to the company headquarters' dug-out.

    Question:

    What does the word 'blundered' reveal about the way the speaker descended the stairs? (2 marks)

3. A lonely boy was reading near a feeble fire.

    Question:

    Explain the feelings the word 'feeble' arouses in the reader compared with a word like 'small'. (2 marks)

4. I swung the door open and hoisted my bad leg over the door sill onto the pavement.

    Question:

    What does the choice of 'hoisted' reveal about the way the narrator moved his leg? (2 marks)

5. My guest was lying sprawled on his back. There was a long knife through his heart which skewered him to the floor.

    Questions:

    (a) *What does the word 'sprawled' add to the picture of the way in which the man's body was lying? (1 mark)*

    (b) *Explain how the word 'skewered' adds to the horror of the scene. (2 marks)*

6. Tom cringed as Mr Connor leaned towards him.

    Question:

    What does 'cringed' tell us about the relationship between the two characters in this extract? (2 marks)

7. The figure was shrouded in a garment of deepest black which concealed its head, its face, its form and left nothing of it visible except one outstretched hand.

    Questions:

    (a) *What associations does the choice of 'shrouded' add to this scene? (1 mark)*

    (b) *Compare the alternatives 'covered' or 'cloaked' instead. (2 marks)*

8. A street urchin gnawed on the remains of a hamburger he had retrieved from a bin.

   Question:

   How does the choice of 'gnawed' help you understand how the child ate? (2 marks)

Word choice to create atmosphere.

Very often, a writer will try to create a particular effect by using many words which have the same sort of meaning. Travel brochures, for example, specialise in trying to make their resorts sound appealing:

> Hastings is not only a fabulous resort but is of course linked to the best known date in history, 1066. From the year of this most famous battle of all time, the region has been acquiring a greater wealth of history and fascination than can be found anywhere else in the country. Within comfortably short journey times you will discover magnificent castles, ancient towns steeped in over a thousand years of history and pretty villages with famous pasts. All linked by glorious rolling countryside with welcoming old world pubs and restaurants along the way.

♦ Discuss:

   How does this writer put over a positive impression of the place he is describing? Pick out all the words and phrases that imply this place is either unique or the best of its kind.

For Practice

1. *(The narrator is a soldier in the first world war.)*

    Back in the main trench, I stood on the fire-step to watch the sky whitening. <u>Sad</u> and <u>stricken</u> the country emerged. I could see the <u>ruined village</u> below the hill and the <u>leafless trees</u> that waited like sentries up by Contalmaison. Down in the craters the <u>dead water</u> took a <u>dull gleam</u> from the sky. I stared at the <u>tangles of wire</u> and the leaning posts, and there seemed <u>no sort of comfort left in life</u>. My <u>steel hat</u> was <u>heavy on my head</u> while I thought how I'd been on leave last month.

    Questions:

    (a) *What kind of atmosphere is created by the use of the words and expressions underlined? (2 marks)*

    (b) *Pick out any **three** expressions and explain precisely what each contributes to this effect. (3 marks)*

2. *(A family newly arrived in Greece from Britain see a house which they may rent.)*

    A gentle curve of hillside rose from the glittering sea. The hill and the valleys around it were <u>an eiderdown of olive-groves</u> that shone with a fish-like gleam where the breeze touched the leaves. Half-way up the slope, <u>guarded by a group of tall, slim cypress-trees</u>, nestled a small strawberry-pink villa, like some exotic fruit lying in the greenery. The cypress-trees undulated gently in the breeze, as if they were busily painting the sky a still brighter blue for our arrival.

    Questions:

    (a) *Explain how each of the two underlined phrases contributes to the sense that the new house will be a refuge to the family. (4 marks)*

    (b) *Pick out **two** other expressions which also add to the attractive nature of the description by appealing to the senses. Explain which of the senses is being appealed to. (4 marks)*

3. (This is the opening sentence of an essay in which the narrator is about to witness an execution.)

    It was in Burma, a sodden morning of the rains. A sickly light, like yellow tinfoil, was slanting over the high walls into the jail yard.

    Questions:

    (a) *Pick out any **two** phrases and show how they help create an uneasy, eerie feeling. (4 marks)*

    (b) *What hints do you think this opening description gives to the writer's feelings about the execution at this point? (2 marks)*

4. I gazed upon the schoolroom into which he took me, as the most forlorn and desolate place I had ever seen. I see it now. A long room, with three long rows of desks, and six of forms, and bristling all round with pegs for hats and slates. Scraps of old copybooks and exercises litter the dirty floor. There is a strange unwholesome smell upon the room, like mildewed corduroys, sweet apples wanting[1] air, and rotten books.

    [1]wanting: lacking

    Question:

    Describe the atmosphere of the schoolroom which the writer builds up. You should refer to at least 5 of the underlined expressions. (5 marks)

5. Over the island the build-up of clouds continued. A steady current of heated air rose all day from the mountain and thrust to ten thousand feet; revolving masses of gas piled up the static until the air was ready to explode. By early evening the sun had gone and a brassy glare had taken the place of clear daylight. Even the air that pushed in from the sea was hot and held no refreshment. Colours drained from water and trees and pink surfaces of rock, and the white and brown clouds brooded.

Question:

Underline or list all the expressions which you feel give a sense of tension building up. (5 marks)

Emotive Language

If a writer is talking about something tragic, such as a disaster, he will use many words which stir up strong emotions. This is known as **emotive** language. For example, the words 'shocking', 'horrifying' and 'appalling' express stronger feelings than words such as 'disturbing', 'worrying' or 'upsetting'. A writer would use the former words to play on the emotions of his readers.

For Practice

Read the following front page newspaper article.

Mortality rate in deprived areas up to twice that of more affluent parts.

POVERTY CAN KILL

Being poor can cost you your life. True. Shocking new statistics released yesterday reveal the monstrous unfairness that blights the future of many of Scotland's citizens. Certain areas of Glasgow have the mortality rate of a third world country, according to information from official government sources.

According to the statistics, people living in multiply deprived Pollock are dying at twice the rate of those who have homes in prosperous Milngavie and Bearsden just a few miles distant as the crow flies.

The figures exposed a deeply disturbing divide between the haves and the have-nots. Your new-born baby is twice as likely to survive into a healthy childhood if you have the right postcode. The wean who enters the world in Springburn or Drumchapel has twice the chance of suffering from heart disease, diabetes and mental illness, and more than three times the likelihood of encountering drug and alcohol related problems.

Initiatives funded by the government to encourage Scots from all walks of life to improve their diet, stop smoking and cut down alcohol intake, have clearly totally and utterly failed to reach the very sections of the population which are most in need of help.

Yesterday politicians of all parties expressed outrage at the blatant inequality in the nation's health situation. They all feared that the deprived areas would remain rooted at the bottom of the health league tables for many more years unless immediate and radical action was taken by the Scottish Executive.

The Scottish Executive described the evidence of the divide in our nation's health as 'worrying' but claimed the root cause of the situation lay with the callous indifference of the previous Conservative administration to the plight of the poor and underprivileged.

♦ Pick out all the words and expressions which you feel have an emotive effect. Then explain what emotions you feel they arouse in the reader.

Writers may use **technical, formal** language if they wish to appear impressively knowledgeable. This is sometimes known as **jargon**, especially when it is used to excess.

Here is an example from a computer handbook. All the examples of jargon are underlined:

> When you finish specifying the <u>typesizes</u> you want, you can <u>preview</u> the effects by choosing the <u>Apply button</u>. The <u>equation</u> is <u>reformatted</u> with the new sizes, but the change is not permanent. If the <u>dialog box</u> is covering your equation, <u>drag</u> the dialog box's <u>title bar</u> to move the box aside.

A writer who wishes to create a setting in a past age may use **archaisms** — deliberately old-fashioned words. Archaisms include expressions such as 'good morrow' for 'good morning' or 'farewell' instead of 'goodbye'. Verb forms such as 'doth' and 'hath' may be used instead of 'does' and 'has'. English that was *actually* written a hundred years ago or more will have many differences from modern day English.

For Practice

1.   Look at the following example:

> A soft answer turneth away wrath; but grievous words stir up anger. The tongue of the wise useth knowledge aright; but the mouth of fools poureth out foolishness.

   ◆   Pick out all the words or expressions which are old-fashioned. Then try to think of how we would now express the same thing in Modern English.

2. The following is an extract from a legal document from an insurance company.

> If any recurring premiums payable cease to be payable the number of ordinary units allocated to the policy immediately after the date of cessation will be unaltered but the number of initial units allocated will be reduced in accordance with provision 2.55 if appropriate.

♦ What do you notice about the number of personal pronouns used?

♦ Usually we avoid repeating words to achieve good style. What is the case here?

♦ What do you notice about the length of the sentence and the number of punctuation marks used?

3. Figures of Speech

A 'figure' of speech is simply an elaborate way of saying something. It might involve comparing one thing to another, or exaggerating something. In Intermediate English, it is not *essential* that you know the technical terms for these, only that you recognise how they work. However, it is helpful and saves time if you do know the terms.

Remember! As with sentence structure and word choice, you will *never* be asked simply to identify a figure of speech such as a simile. You will always be asked to explain the *effect* it has.

Literal / Figurative language

The word 'literal' means the actual thing; 'figurative' is something suggested by a figure of speech.

Beware of the common mistake which is to think 'literally' means 'definitely'.

Look at this example :

'The audience were literally glued to their seats' .

If this were *literally* true, it would mean that all the members of the audience were stuck down to their seats with glue. To say someone is 'glued to his seat' is a **metaphor**.

What the writer *actually* meant was that the audience were so interested no one moved or dreamed of getting up to leave. In fact they were **metaphorically** or **figuratively** glued to their seats.

- A **metaphor** is a comparison of one thing to another which is basically unlike it, but has something in common with it.

- A **simile** is a similar figure of speech involving comparison, but it actually includes the words 'like' or 'as'.

- **Personification** is a comparison of something to a person.

- The term **image** is used to describe the thing that the subject is being compared to.

You will be required to give an explanation of how effective the image is. Remember to *identify* the image — in other words, say what is being compared to what. Look at these examples:

Example 1

In Shakespeare's *Romeo and Juliet*, Romeo says,

'Juliet is the sun'.

This simple but effective image suggests how bright and beautiful she seems to him, eclipsing all the other girls, just as the sun is the brightest object in the sky. It also suggests she is far away from him and perhaps seems unobtainable at this point.

Example 2

The Empire State Building, that jumbo-size dentist's drill

This metaphor from Norman MacCaig's poem *Hotel Room, 12th Floor* is effective because it is so surprising. The image of a dentist's drill suggests the long, pointed shape of the building, but it also has overtones of pain, which is appropriate as MacCaig focuses on the violence in New York in this poem. The expression 'jumbo-size' is comical as it is associated with marketing, which hints at the commercialised nature of the city, and also the fact that in America everything is supposedly 'bigger and better'.

Figures focusing on Sound

♦ **Alliteration** (repetition of consonant sounds) is often used to increase the impact of a phrase. You should try to focus on the actual sound itself and the effect the writer is trying to achieve. The alliteration of Lady Macbeth's words after the murder of Duncan: 'I heard the owl scream and the crickets cry' is effective because of the harsh abrasive 'cr' sound, which is a nerve-grating sound like finger nails on a wall, which perfectly expresses the high tension of the moment.

♦ **Assonance** is the precise term for a similar repetition of vowel sounds, e.g., 'doomed youth'.

♦ **Onomatopoeia** is the term used for sounds which imitate the sense like 'buzz' and 'hiss'.

Other Figures of Speech

♦ **Hyperbole** (or exaggeration) is a very common figure of speech which candidates often fail to notice in examinations. When you say 'I've been there hundreds of times' you actually mean a large number of times. Using hyperbole emphasises the frequency. Very often hyperbole is used for comic effect: 'his eyes popped out of his head'. Look at Close Reading test number 3 for many examples of this.

- ♦ **Understatement** is the opposite of hyperbole, and achieves its effect in an ironic way. 'He was not very happy' can often mean 'He was extremely angry'. The effect may be humorous, or it may contribute to suspense.

- ♦ **Euphemism** is a way of expressing something in a gentler way than the harsh truth. Many euphemisms are associated with death, e.g., 'My old dog was put to sleep.'

For Practice

Answer the questions on the following examples which all focus on figures of speech.

1. The little low-ceilinged cabin below was rather larger than a hearse, and as dark as a vault. It had two coffins on each side — I mean two bunks. A small table, capable of accommodating three persons at dinner, stood against the forward bulkhead, and over it hung the dingiest whale-oil lantern that ever peopled the obscurity of a dungeon with ghostly shapes. The floor room unoccupied was not extensive. One might swing a cat in it, perhaps, but not a long cat.

   Question:

   *Show how the writer uses **comparisons, imagery** and **understatement** to suggest the tiny cabin in this old boat is claustrophobic and unsafe. (10 marks)*

2. I forgot to say that the noise made by the bubbling lava is not great, heard as we heard it from the look-out house. It makes three distinct sounds — a rushing, a hissing, and a coughing or puffing sound; and if you stand on the brink and close your eyes it is not hard at all to imagine you are sweeping down a river on a large low-pressure paddle-steamer, and that you hear the hissing of the steam about her boilers, the puffing from her escape-pipes and the churning rush of the water around her paddles.

   Question:

   *Pick out one example of **onomatopoeia** and one example of **assonance** in this extract and explain the effect of each. (4 marks)*

3. My companion went for the soup of the day, which was about three spoonfuls of a milky mushroom soup just visible at the bottom of a bowl. As music from *Evita* warbled its way round the room, I found myself looking at a tiny portion of sea bass, measuring about 2 × 3 in, so small that one could probably have carved it off the fish while it was swimming along without it ever noticing.

   Question:

   *Show how the writer uses **hyperbole** to achieve a humorous effect in writing a critical review of this restaurant. (4 marks)*

4. They'll take suggestion as a cat laps milk.

   Question:

   *In this quotation from Shakespeare's 'The Tempest', two villains are planning to trick two other characters. Explain how this **simile** reveals the speaker is very confident they will succeed. (2 marks)*

5. The old man was looking at me with blazing eyes.

   'He is safe,' he cried. 'You cannot follow in time . . . He is gone . . . he has triumphed . . .'

   There was more in those eyes than any common triumph. They had been hooded like a bird of prey, and now they flamed with a hawk's pride. A white fanatic heat burned in them, and I realised for the first time the terrible thing I had been up against.

   Question:

   *Pick out all the words which suggest **images** of a bird of prey and fire. How do these images help you to imagine the character of the old man? (4 marks)*

6. Farfrae and Lucetta might have been seen flitting about the town like two butterflies — or rather like a bee and a butterfly.

   Question:

   *What impression do you get of the couple from the first **simile** 'like two butterflies'? What difference does the change of simile after the dash make to this impression?(3 marks)*

7. To her horror and amazement, round the bend of the river she saw a shaggy, tawny wave-front of water advancing like a wall of lions.

   Question:

   *The writer is describing the tidal wave of muddy water following a dam bursting. To what extent is the **image** of the 'wall of lions' effective? (3 marks)*

8. Dr No came slowly out from behind the desk and moved towards them. He seemed to glide rather than take steps. His knees did not dent the matt, gunmetal sheen of his kimono and no shoes showed below the sweeping hem. It was impossible to tell Doctor No's age: as far as Bond could see, there were no lines on the face. The eyebrows were fine and black and sharply upswept as if they had been painted on as make-up for a conjurer. Below them, slanting jet black eyes stared out of the skull. They were without eyelashes. They looked like the mouths of two small revolvers, direct and unblinking and totally devoid of expression. The bizarre, gliding figure looked like a giant venomous worm wrapped in grey tin-foil, and Bond would not have been surprised to see the rest of it trailing slimily along the carpet behind.

   DR NO by Ian Fleming © Glidrose Productions Ltd., 1958

   Question:

   *Show how the writer has used **imagery** effectively to make the character of Dr No seem a terrifying opponent for James Bond. (6 marks)*

4. Structure of a Text

The word 'structure' suggests a building. Just as a building is carefully constructed with bricks and mortar on top of a foundation, so a piece of writing will have an introduction, a main text and a conclusion. The various parts of the text will be linked by words, phrases and sentences which act as the 'mortar'.

Introductions

Introductions can be presented in various ways, but the purpose is always the same: to give the reader a general idea of the topic which is to be explored. Sometimes the topic will be introduced in a straightforward manner. At other times a writer may choose to begin the text with an anecdote (short story) which illustrates the topic or with a piece of conversation. A question or series of questions may be posed to start the reader thinking.

♦ Look at the pieces of writing on pages 66, 71 and 77. In each case, the writer has chosen a different method of introduction. Can you decide in each case what has been chosen?

Linkage

Various 'markers' will link the stages of the argument. These could be conjunctions or phrases like 'but', 'yet' or 'on the other hand' which mark a change in direction. If an argument is to be added to, expressions like 'furthermore', 'moreover', 'a further advantage' or 'in addition' will point to this. Sometimes a whole sentence will be used to mark a turning point, and you may be asked a question on this.

The simplest question you will be asked about linkage is:

> What is the function of this sentence in the argument?

Such a question would be worth 1 mark.

The answer, obviously, is that it **forms a link**.

However, you might be asked to show *how* it forms a link.

Look at the following example:

Following the Roman invasion in 43 AD, the south of Britain was totally subdued within thirty years; many Britons were sold as slaves and the land was covered with Roman roads and towns. Soon, south Britain was to be a complete Roman province, the townsmen speaking Latin and building for themselves those comfortable Roman houses with central heating. A Roman temple to the god Mithras has been excavated in the heart of London. <u>But, unlike their easy victory in the south, the north of the country resisted the foreign invaders</u>. Here the Romans were never able to do more than hold down the natives for short periods. There were no Roman towns, no country houses, no temples, only forts and camps where soldiers lived for a time.

Question: How does the sentence underlined form a link in the argument?

The accepted method for doing this is to pick out the parts of the sentence that sum up the two ideas to be linked. You must *quote* these, and then explain **in your own words** the ideas they are referring to, making clear which idea comes before the linking sentence and which follows. In the above example the two parts of the sentence which provide the link are 'easy victory in the south' and 'the north of the country resisted'.

The answer should read:

> The words 'easy victory in the south' refer to the Romans' quick transformation of Southern Britain which is discussed in the first part of the paragraph. The words 'the north of the country resisted' link to the next idea which describes how little the Romans were able to achieve in the north.

For Practice

Using the method explained on the previous page, show how each of the underlined sentences in the following extracts act as a link. Each question is worth 2 marks.

1. When the sun sank down it was luxury to sit in the perfumed air and forget that there was any world but these enchanted islands. <u>It was such ecstasy to dream, and dream — till you got a bite.</u> A scorpion bite. Then the first duty was to get up out of the grass and kill the scorpion; and the next to bathe the bitten place with alcohol and the next to resolve to keep out of the grass in future.

2. In Madras, as in other garrison towns in India, there were many orphan children of soldiers who had been killed, or died of disease, or had been unaware that they had a child. These children faced an unenviable future. In the Hindu community of their mothers they were unacceptable and in the European community they were equally unacceptable because of their native upbringing.

3. When more coal was needed, men dug tunnels into the earth from the quarries. This was dangerous work, because the earth was always falling into the tunnel. Later they dug deeper and this brought greater difficulties and greater danger. Water seeped into the bottom of the pits, poisonous and explosive gases collected, and taking the coal to the surface was hard work. Slowly the dangers were overcome. Miners became more skilful at supporting the roofs of the tunnels, and engineers began to use steam engines to pump the water out. They lit fires at the bottom of pit shafts to drive out foul air; and Sir Humphry Davy invented a lamp which would not set fire to explosive gases.

4. After 1750 the coming of the new steam-driven machines brought an end to the old way of life in many towns. Factories and houses were put up as cheaply and as quickly as possible without any thought for the health of the townsfolk. For a long time town councils had tried to keep the towns clean but they had not been very successful. Many councils, too, simply elected themselves year after year and did not bother their heads about such things. All this did not matter very much while the towns were small but after they began to grow rapidly it became a very serious problem indeed. Many diseases such as cholera, caused by filth and lack of sanitation, swept through the dirty overcrowded houses of the factory towns and killed thousands of people every year.

5. The earliest part of Madras College was opened in 1833. It was designed by William Burn, one of the leading architects of his time in Scotland. The cloistered quadrangle and the little bell towers suggest mediaeval church architecture. At first the quadrangle was unpaved and became a muddy mess in wet weather. In 1843 it was drained and the Caithness stone slabs which still remain were laid in a bed of lime. <u>With one exception the school buildings as they were to remain for the next century were complete</u>. The exception was the building at present used to house Commerce and History. It was erected in 1864 to meet a particular need. Although the school had been coeducational from the beginning, many parents of girls were not happy for their daughters to attend open classes. The trustees provided this building for the 'sheltered schooling and teaching by selected masters to young ladies'.

5. Tone

You may be asked a specific question on tone, or tone may be included in the list of choices to discuss in the Evaluation questions. The tone of a piece of writing reflects the attitude of the writer to his subject. It is possibly easiest to imagine it in spoken English. The words 'Very nice' might be said warmly and sincerely to a friend who has just given you the present you always wanted. But how would you say it if you opened the present and you didn't know what the thing was? Politely? Cautiously? The same words could be said sarcastically, ironically or even bitterly if a good friend had forgotten to give you anything at all!

To decide on the tone, it can be helpful to try to decide what the writer's purpose is. Is he being funny or serious? Is he trying to stir up some sort of feeling in his reader? Is he trying to persuade the reader to believe in a point of view?

Examples of tone

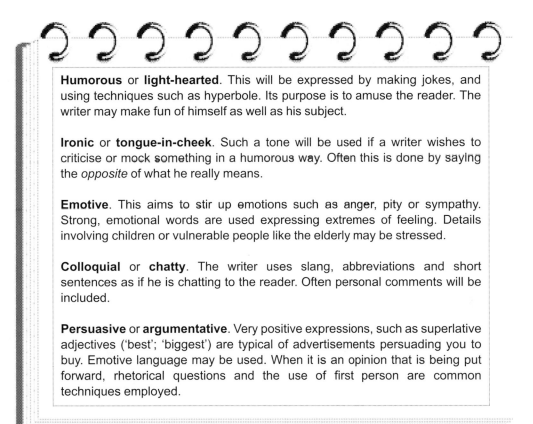

Humorous or **light-hearted**. This will be expressed by making jokes, and using techniques such as hyperbole. Its purpose is to amuse the reader. The writer may make fun of himself as well as his subject.

Ironic or **tongue-in-cheek**. Such a tone will be used if a writer wishes to criticise or mock something in a humorous way. Often this is done by saying the *opposite* of what he really means.

Emotive. This aims to stir up emotions such as anger, pity or sympathy. Strong, emotional words are used expressing extremes of feeling. Details involving children or vulnerable people like the elderly may be stressed.

Colloquial or **chatty**. The writer uses slang, abbreviations and short sentences as if he is chatting to the reader. Often personal comments will be included.

Persuasive or **argumentative**. Very positive expressions, such as superlative adjectives ('best'; 'biggest') are typical of advertisements persuading you to buy. Emotive language may be used. When it is an opinion that is being put forward, rhetorical questions and the use of first person are common techniques employed.

For Practice

The following extracts are examples of the five types of tone listed in the box on the previous page. Can you identify which is which?

1.   **Terror of Hijack Jet Passengers.**

Twelve gunmen who hijacked a jet subjected passengers to a terrifying five-day ordeal. Shortly after the flight took off from Kabul, Afghanistan, the men forced the pilot to divert to Stansted Airport. When the aircraft landed, they threatened to kill the 173 passengers — who included 21 children and a heavily pregnant woman — and blow up the aircraft unless they were granted asylum. The hijackers — who were heavily armed with hand grenades, loaded handguns and knives and knuckle-dusters — made repeated threats to kill passengers. A steward was beaten up and left on the tarmac with his hands tied behind his back. Passengers were ordered to keep their heads down and not to look up on pain of death.

2.   In the morning I went to Elvis Presley's birthplace. A path behind the house led to a gift shop where you could buy Elvis memorabilia — albums, badges, plates, posters. There was a visitors' book by the door. The book had a column for remarks. Reading down the list they said, 'Nice', 'Real nice', 'Very nice', 'Nice'. Such eloquence.

3.   You don't build a reputation like the University's for no apparent reason. In fact, we believe that it's our devotion to quality and excellence for the last 400 years that has gained us this position. It's a position we are proud of and one we will do everything to respect. Especially these days, with more and more emphasis on quality, the University remains committed to excellence above everything else.

4. **Star Wars** (1977). A technically dazzling and enjoyable science fiction film for children of all ages. The plot is the bad guys (the galactic empire) vs the good guys (the rebels). You'll root for the good guys and hope the beautiful young princess will be rescued by two young Prince Charmings. You'll still enjoy the film on TV.

5. My father, when behind the wheel, was more or less permanently lost. Most of the time he was just kind of lost, but whenever we got near something we were intent on seeing he would become seriously lost. Generally it would take him about an hour to realise that he had gone from the first stage to the second. All during that time, as he blundered through some unfamiliar city, making sudden and unpredictable turns, getting honked at for going the wrong way down one-way streets or for hesitating in the middle of busy intersections, my mother would mildly suggest that perhaps we should pull over and ask directions. But my father would pretend not to hear her and would press on in that semi-obsessional state that tends to overcome fathers when things aren't going well.

   Eventually, after driving the wrong way down the same one-way street so many times that merchants were beginning to come and watch from their doorways, Dad would stop the car and gravely announce, 'Well, I think we should ask directions', in a tone suggesting that this had been his desire all along.

© Bill Bryson 1989.

EVALUATION

To answer Evaluation questions, you must consider **how effectively** the writer has presented his information. You must express your personal response to the text. You might get this across by using the pronoun 'I' as in 'I particularly liked the simile in line . . . as I felt it expressed . . .'.

You can also express your judgement by using words like **effective, moving, satisfying, exciting, interesting, amusing, humorous, convincing, persuasive, shocking, disturbing, entertaining, enjoyable** and so on. Whenever you use a word of this type you are expressing a response to the writer's technique.

Very often, an Evaluation question will be broken down into topics which you may choose from. For example, in the final Evaluation question in the 2000 Intermediate 2 paper, candidates were given the following selection:

> **Giving examples to support your answer**, explain how the writer has used **any three** of the following features . . .
>
> - ◆ Figures of speech.
> - ◆ Word choice, including the use of technical terms.
> - ◆ Structure and / or word order.
> - ◆ Techniques of argument such as illustration, comparison, contrast, proof and disproof.
> - ◆ The style, tone or register adopted.
> - ◆ Humour.

This question was worth 6 marks. What was wanted was a balanced answer with each of the three topics being dealt with in reasonable detail, with perhaps two quotations for each. It is a good idea to **write down the titles** of the features you have chosen and underline them as **sub-headings**. The examiner will then have a clear idea of what you are trying to do, and it is likely you will be able to think through your answer more clearly.

Another Evaluation question was more general. It asked your opinion of the conclusion.

> Giving reasons for your answer, explain how effectively you think lines . . . **round off** the article. (4 marks)

To show how a conclusion rounds off a text, you must consider:

♦ The **ideas**: pick out references to stages in the argument from the rest of the text. Does the passage end with the argument having been clearly resolved, or is the outcome undecided? Is there some sort of **twist** or something unexpected?

♦ The **style**: note whether the style remains the same or changes from the rest of the passage. Often a conclusion will return to the wording of the opening paragraph. An image used at the start may be used again in a slightly different form. **Word choice** and **sentence structure** could be discussed under this heading, but they must be related to the rest of the passage.

♦ The **tone**: note if the tone remains the same. Does it become serious after a light-hearted discussion, or does it end on a light-hearted note?

♦ The **punch-line**: is there some sort of joke which gives the conclusion particular impact? Some writers may use a quotation or even introduce a new idea which leaves food for thought.

Checklist for Evaluation questions

◆ Note the **number of marks** available and tailor your answer to suit.

◆ Be sure to **follow the instructions**: e.g., choose **three** features.

◆ Clearly write down as **sub-headings** the titles of the features you choose to discuss.

◆ Use **quotations** or **examples** to illustrate your answer.

PART TWO:

PASSAGES
for
CLOSE READING

The following exercises are based on the format for Intermediate 2.

The short additional exercises following each text could be done orally, in groups or as individual extra tests of the aspects highlighted.

1. WATERY GRAVE ROBBERS

At the beginning of the nineteenth century, the murderous exploits of Burke and Hare were the culmination of a brisk trade in dead bodies for the medical schools of Scotland. Freelance journalist Jeremy Hodges tells the story.

On the opening of the Union Canal in 1822, horse-drawn boats could cross Scotland with ease, carrying cargoes of freight and human passengers — alive or dead.

5   The grim secret trade went largely undetected, but for its first decade the new fast route was a watery highway of horror. Bodies snatched from graveyards were smuggled away to the expanding medical schools in Edinburgh and Glasgow.

  Without a steady supply of corpses for dissection, would-be doctors and surgeons could not be trained in anatomy — and there were more than 1,000

10   medical students in Edinburgh alone. Since corpses — or 'subjects', as the anatomy lecturers preferred to call them — could rarely be obtained legally, they fetched a good price, with no questions asked. Many shady characters were happy to violate a sepulchre for up to £1,000 in today's money.

  The most convenient graveyards were near the canal. In 1829, a poor blind

15   orphan boy of 12 was buried in the remote Chapel-yard at Bonnybridge, near Falkirk. The boy had been a familiar face along the canal, playing his violin to entertain travellers on the passenger boats. But tragedy struck when he was invited to play at a party one night in Dennyloanhead. Walking home alone, he fell into the canal and drowned. His body was recovered and buried in the

20   Chapel-yard, separated only by a low stone wall from the Forth and Clyde Canal.

  The boy's blindness made him an interesting 'subject' for dissection. According to a contemporary newspaper account: 'The boy's friends had taken every precaution to prevent his grave being violated. It was dug deep

25   and the coffin of his father, who had been buried in the same spot some years before, was lifted and placed above that of his son.'

But all to no avail. A week later, as a luggage boat was passing Bonnybridge, two men put a large box on board with directions that it would be collected at Port Dundas, Glasgow. During the journey the boat's captain became
30   suspicious, and decided to check the box's contents. On forcing off the lid, the horrified man found himself confronted by a familiar young face. The captain alerted the police in Glasgow and, when two men appeared to collect the box, one was apprehended while the other fled. The boy's body was returned to a relative in Falkirk and given a decent burial once more.

35   Yet even such desperate stratagems could not keep the medical schools supplied. Many of the bodies transported by canal to Edinburgh came from Ireland, via Liverpool and Glasgow. Such was the poverty in Ireland, corpses could be purchased for ten shillings. In Edinburgh they fetched £10.

The scandal that eventually helped end the grisly trade was the work of two
40   Irish navvies who came to Scotland to work on the Union canal. From 1818 to 1822, William Burke worked on the Falkirk stretch of the project and William Hare was employed at the Edinburgh end of the canal. It may be that he learned the nasty secrets of some of the barrels and boxes — and their ultimate destination. After Burke came by chance to lodge with him in 1827,
45   the pair lost little time in making the acquaintance of Robert Knox, who had 500 anatomy students in his classes. Knox spent £800 — around £80,000 in today's money —- on 'subjects', amounting to maybe 1,000 bodies. He once lost £200 paid in advance for corpses from Ireland which he never received. He was no more unscrupulous than the other anatomists — he just happened
50   to be implicated in one of the most notorious criminal trials in history.

When Burke and Hare supplied him with their first murder victim, Knox asked no questions and complimented them on the body's freshness. They needed no further encouragement. During 1828, at least 16 men, women and children were suffocated, stripped and dumped in tea chests or herring barrels and
55   carted round to Surgeons' Square. When they were caught, Hare turned King's Evidence and Burke was hanged. His body was subjected to public dissection by Knox's rival, Professor Alexander Monro, as a howling mob of medical students bayed for admission to the packed anatomical theatre and smashed the windows.

60   The scandalous publicity thrust upon this unlovely aspect of medical science was a powerful factor in influencing parliament to pass the Anatomy Act three years later. From then, enough anatomical 'subjects' could be obtained legally from the poor houses — and the grim trade on Scotland's canals came to an end.

QUESTIONS

Mark Code

1. Explain **two** ways in which the word 'dead' (line 3) stands out in the first paragraph.   2   A

2. 'A watery highway of horror' (line 5)

   (a) Explain **in your own words** what the writer means by this expression.   2   U

   (b) Suggest any **one** way in which the writer has made this phrase striking to the reader.   1   A

3. Give **two** reasons from lines 1–13 for large numbers of bodies being 'snatched' from graveyards at this period.   2   U

4. 'subjects' as the anatomy lecturers preferred to call them. (lines 10–11)

   Suggest a reason **why** the anatomy lecturers preferred to call the corpses 'subjects'.   2   A

5. (a) Pick out any **two** words or expressions used in lines 14–15 to describe the boy who played the violin which particularly build up sympathy for him.

   Explain how each of the words or expressions you have chosen arouses your sympathy for the boy.   2   A

   (b) Explain in your own words why the grave-robbers were particularly keen to obtain this particular boy's body.   2   U

   (c) Give two reasons why this boy's body would be difficult for the body-snatchers to obtain and one reason why it would be easy for them.   3   U

6. 'But all to no avail'. (line 27)

   Show how this sentence acts as a link in the story of the blind boy.   2   A

7. Burke and Hare moved on from stealing bodies that were already dead to murdering people in order to sell their bodies. What do the words 'dumped' (line 54) and 'carted' (line 55) suggest about their attitude to their victims?　　2　　A

8. 'up to £1,000 in today's money' (line 13); around £80,000 in today's money (lines 46–47).

   Suggest a reason why the writer gives these payments for bodies in 'today's money'.　　1　　A

9. Look at the description of the reaction of the medical students in lines 57–59.

   'howling' in line 57 suggests the angry medical students made a noise like a pack of hounds. What other word in this paragraph continues this idea?　　1　　A

10. Look at the role of Dr Robert Knox, the Professor of Anatomy in the story (lines 44–end). Referring closely to the text in your answer, show whether you feel the writer intends us to approve or disapprove of Dr Knox.　　2　　A

11. Giving examples to support your answer, show how the writer has used any two of the following to emphasise the horror of the story of the trade in human bodies:

   　　word choice;
   　　figures of speech;
   　　use of examples;
   　　use of contrast and comparison;
   　　structure of the argument.　　6　　E

Total marks　(30)

FOCUS ON STRUCTURE

The argument in the passage 'Watery Grave Robbers' was carefully structured. The following extra questions will help you to be aware of the techniques the writer has used.

Marks

1. The passage opens with a reference to the opening of the Union Canal. What is the connection between this event and the rest of the story? 2

2. Read lines 1–13. Which one sentence best sums up what the first part of the story is about? 1

3. Look at the second section of the story (lines 14–34). Explain clearly how this section relates to the opening one. 2

4. Look at the seventh paragraph (lines 35–38). A new development in the story is described.

   What is this new development? 1

5. Show how the sentence 'Yet . . . supplied' acts as a link at this stage. 2

6. The last section describes the murderers, Burke and Hare.

   What phrase in the opening sentence of the eighth paragraph (lines 39–50) suggests that this will be the conclusion to the topic. 1

7. *(a)* What new topic is introduced in the final paragraph to round off the article? 1

   (b) Explain how this provides an effective conclusion to the article. 2

Total marks (12)

2.   THE MIXED BLESSING OF ETERNAL LIFE

Should the young be given priority over the old in the allocation of National Health Service resources? Journalist Colette Douglas Home argues that they should in this article from 'The Daily Mail'.

The father of a friend once said to me: 'You can live too long.' He was 90 and lonely as a unicorn. His friends were dead, his family scattered. This tall, spare old man spent his endless days in the reference library learning facts he no longer had use for; or playing the stock exchange with money he no longer
5   valued. He was itching for death.

For most of us I suspect it will get that way. We, the longest-lived generation yet. We, who may be in the right place at the right time to benefit from a sort of immortality offered by genome science. Who was it who said that when the Gods wish to be cruel they grant our prayers? Man has always yearned for
10   eternal life — but will it be to his taste?

Perhaps it is because I think it will not, that I find it hard to be shocked by the Ayrshire GP who said he thought the young should take precedence over the old if health service resources had to be rationed. Far from being shocked I rather presumed it was an attitude that had always prevailed.

15   That is not to say that the medical profession practises euthanasia by stealth. It is merely to suspect that physicians of great compassion and long experience marry quality with quantity when they judge how far to intervene between patients and their natural end. They may have a patient whose cancer has returned for the third, fourth or fifth time. They could recommend
20   heroic surgery or a blitz of chemotherapy.

Such treatment would prolong life. If the patient was 20 years old with a small dependent child no doctor would count the cost to NHS resources. But what if the patient was 89, arthritic, worn out by the daily struggle and confined to a nursing home? Would the treatment be appropriate? Should the doctor
25   proceed without counting the cost — both human and financial?

The older generation are a canny bunch. They budgeted their way through times harder than we have ever known. They also have a clear-eyed understanding of the natural process. I dare say many of them would decide against treatment if the decision was theirs.

30   The hard fact is that God or nature or whatever accident of fate produced us designed us with a given life span. Death is part of the package and (barring tragedy and accident) death is supposed to be the lot of the old, not the young.

Our biblical span was three score years and ten. We have stretched that. We
35   have added a decade. But we have postponed the inevitable, not eradicated it. Those of us with any sense prepare to accept that with all the grace we can muster.

Bearing that in mind, if there was a genuine shortage of resources in the NHS, which of us would muscle past the young to the front of the queue? The longer
40   we keep people alive the more medical intervention they need. The elderly get a big slice of NHS resources. This is right and proper. No one is suggesting they should receive second class treatment. But, meanwhile, at the other end of the age range, more new and radical procedures are being developed to enhance the lives of the unwell young. And there are finite
45   resources.

So let us be realistic. While money remains inelastic, choices have to be made. They cannot always be determined by extremity of illness. That leaves age. So long as care and compassion rule the decision, it seems to me that nature set the precedent for the choice. And, as I said at the beginning, the
50   very, very old often come to the conclusion that we can live too long.

© Colette Douglas Home

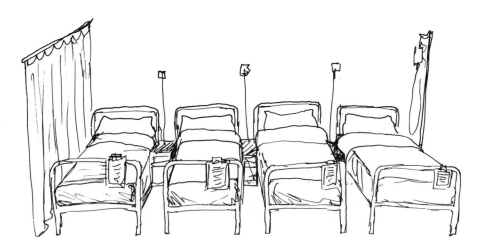

QUESTIONS

1. Read lines 1–5. 'The father . . . for death'.

    In your own words, give **two** reasons why the old man was so lonely.   2   U

2. 'We. . . .science.' (lines 6–8)

    Show how the author uses **sentence structure** to express her pride in being part of the modern generation.   2   A

3. Read lines 11–14. 'Perhaps . . . prevailed.'

    In your own words, explain how the writer feels about the idea of the Ayrshire GP that young people should be given preference to older people in the allocation of medical treatment.   2   U

4. 'marry quality with quantity'. (line 17)

    What does this phrase suggest doctors should consider when deciding whether to keep a patient alive?   2   U

5. In lines 21–25, the writer compares the circumstances of two patients.

    (a) In your own words, explain **two** of the differences between these patients.   2   U

    (b) The author does not state *directly* that she thinks the second patient should be left to die. Show with close reference to the text how she manages to suggest this without stating it directly.   2   A

6. Read lines 26–29. 'The older generation . . . theirs.'

    (a) Pick out **two** words or expressions (**not** whole sentences) which suggest that the older generation have common sense.   2   U

    (b) Quote the expression that shows the writer is not entirely sure that the elderly *would* choose not to be treated.   1   U

7. 'Death is part of the package'. (line 31)

    (a) Explain what the writer means by this description of human life.   2   U

    (b) Explain how her choice of expression 'part of the package' affects her *tone* here.   2   A

8. 'Our biblical span was three score years and ten'. (line 34)

    Give a reason why the author has used this form of expressing the number instead of simply saying '70 years'.   1   A

9. 'The elderly get a big slice'. (lines 40–41)

    Explain how the **image** the writer uses in this expression helps the reader understand how NHS resources are allocated.   2   A

10. Look again at the first paragraph of the article (lines 1–5).

    Explain, with reference to the passage as a whole, how effective you find this as an introduction.   2   E

11. With reference to any **three** of the following, show how well the writer has succeeded in putting across her argument that old people should not always be given medical treatment to prolong their lives:

        use of first person ('we', 'us', etc.);
        word choice and imagery;
        sentence structure;
        use of examples;
        sense of personal involvement;
        emotive language.   6   E

Total marks (30)

FOCUS ON PERSUASIVE WRITING

The purpose of the passage 'The Mixed Blessing of Eternal Life' is to persuade the reader to share a point of view. The following questions highlight some of the ways in which the writer aims to do this.

Marks

1. Read lines 1–5. The writer begins with an anecdote (small personal story) .

    (a) Quote a phrase which might persuade the reader that the anecdote is true.   1

    (b) Pick **two** expressions which describe the old man which aim to arouse emotions such as pity in the reader.   2

2. 'For most of us I suspect it will get that way'. (line 6)

    Why is the use of 'most of us' more effective at persuading the reader than 'most people' would be?   2

3. Read lines 15–20 'That is not . . . chemotherapy'.

    (a) Pick out **two** phrases the writer uses to describe those doctors whom she believes would stop treating the old.   2

    (b) How does the use of these phrases help strengthen her argument?   1

4. Read lines 34–36 'Our biblical span . . . we can muster'.

    (a) In this paragraph, the writer gives us a reason to be grateful for the length of life we now have. Explain the reason in your own words.   1

    (b) Pick out the phrase which makes the reader want to belong to the group who are grateful.   1

5. Read lines 38–39 'Bearing that in mind . . . queue?'

    What answer does the writer assume the reader will give to the question?   1

6. 'So let us be realistic.'

    Describe the writer's tone in this summing up.   1

Total marks   (12)

♦   Discuss: Sum up the various techniques this writer uses to persuade her readers to accept her argument.

3.   EVEN BEGGARS HAVE CHIPS ON THEIR SHOULDERS

In this article from 'The Scotsman', David Gray describes some encounters with beggars in Scotland's capital.

Extract from true conversation from last Friday, around noon:

Grubby beggar fella sitting on pavement: "Huv ye goat any spare change, Big Man?"

5   Big Man, putting 50p in fella's paper cup: "Thank you." (This is just one of the odd things people say to beggars in mumbling, embarrassed fashion.)

Grubby Fella: "Thanks very much . . . ur ye goan tae the Stones concert tonight, Big Man?"

10   Big Man, with a horrified premonition of what's to follow: "No. Um . . . can't afford it . . . are you, then?"

Grubby Fella: "Aye!"

Big Man: "What?"

Grubby Fella: "It'll be brill . . . shame ye're no comin'."

15   The Big Man leaps on the Grubby Fella and tries to wrest the 50p piece from his grasp, and the two roll around in the street, biting and cursing. OK, the last bit is untrue, but only because I didn't have the nerve; the rest is spot on.

The thing is, it shouldn't have been so upsetting, as once you've handed over the cash, it's none of your business what the recipient does with it . . . if every penny in the cup / hat / outstretched hand / open mouth went on cups of tea or 20   blankets, the poor fellas would spend their entire lives running to the toilet, if they weren't trapped under several hundred kilos of blankets.

A similar lesson was learned one night when, on a late shift, I was delegated to collect a pizza for myself and colleagues. At that time there was an offer that if you ordered a giant pizza you got one of the same for free; thus, brimming

25   with the milk of human kindness, I resolved to donate the spare one to the first beggar I clapped eyes on, something that in Edinburgh usually takes under half a second.

Sure enough, there was a raggedy chap under a blanket a few yards from the door of the pizza place, with a cardboard sign reading "Homeless and hungry.
30   Please help."

"Here you go," I ventured, smiling. The chap stared at the box as if I was handing him a live rattlesnake and shouted: "If I see another pizza ah'm goin tae be seek!"

Not to be deterred, I went in search of worthier persons (after first being
35   obliged to give the pizza-hater a pound), but received various threats, refusals, stony silences and sneering lips, until at last two younger beggars accepted with bad grace, clearly aware that a refusal would have ended in tears (mine).

Of course, just because you're homeless and hungry doesn't necessarily
40   mean you want a pizza, but only in Scotland would the essentially well-meaning offer be taken as an insult. In other countries, it might be assumed that holding a piece of paper saying "hungry" suggests that you would not be surprised by someone offering you food. Had the sign read: "Hungry, but not especially fond of Italian cuisine or anything with olives in it", the reaction might
45   have been understandable.

It's a Scottish thing, though, that even beggars have chips on their shoulders (if not on their hand-written list of acceptable food donations). I once got chased for half a mile for speaking out of turn when a band of the New Age-style beggars decided to take umbrage at the fact that I had, and was using, a
50   mobile phone in public.

The incident took place on a summer evening, walking through Edinburgh's meadows. The crusty posse was sitting on the grass drinking beer and smoking while their little dogs chased each other in circles, tangling the string leads that seem to be very much in vogue. As I walked past, talking, one
55   shouted "Aye, you and yer **** mobile phone, we've no' even got hooses to stay in!"

One of my curses in life being a smart mouth, I shouted back without pausing to do a headcount of the opposition: "What's it to you that I've got a mobile phone? What would you do with one? Who are you going to call? Ye've not
60   even got anywhere to plug it in to charge it anyway!"

Rather than this being met with replies of "fair comment" and "sorry to have screamed abuse at you for nothing", the rabble lurched to its collective feet and headed in my direction, spraying beer and curses.

65 Luckily a smart mouth in Scotland tends to go in tandem with a fast pair of legs (or an early grave), and I was by this time some distance away and accelerating. "If you hadn't eaten so many free pizzas you might be faster," I added, wittily. From a mile away.

© David Gray

QUESTIONS

1. Look at the conversation between the writer and the 'grubby beggar' (lines 2–13).

   Using quotation to support your answer, explain **two** differences between the styles of language used by the two speakers.   4   A

2. Explain why the beggar's words 'shame ye're no comin',' seemed ironic to the writer.   2   U

3. Read lines 14–15. 'The Big Man . . . cursing'.

   In the next sentence the writer admits this part of the story is untrue. Give **one** reason for him choosing to end the story of the encounter in this way, although it is untrue.   2   A

4. Read lines 17–21. 'The thing is . . . kilos of blankets'.

   In your own words, explain why the writer feels he was wrong to be angry with the beggar.   2   U

5. Read lines 39–45. 'Of course . . . have been understandable.'

   Can you suggest a serious point the writer may be making about the beggars who refused the offer of free pizza?   2   A

6. Show how the context helps you understand the meaning of 'take umbrage' in line 49.   2   U

7. Read lines 51–54 'The incident . . . in vogue'.

   Pick out **two** expressions from these lines which might have suggested people would be in a peaceful, happy mood, and explain why each of them has this effect.   2   U

8. The writer could have used 'got' instead of 'lurched' in line 62. Explain what 'lurched' adds to the picture of the beggars.   2   A

9. 'Spraying beer and curses'. (line 63)

   Explain how the word 'spraying' is used both literally and figuratively in this phrase.   4   A

10. Show how the writer uses sentence structure in the last paragraph to achieve a humorous effect.   2   E

11. Looking at the passage as a whole, show how the author reveals his attitude to beggars.

    Discuss his use of **two** of the following:

       direct speech;
       exaggeration (hyperbole);
       use of examples;
       word choice;
       irony;
       humour.   6   E

                                                        Total marks   (30)

FOCUS ON HUMOUR

Humorous writing is more carefully crafted than it often appears. The following questions will help you think about some of the techniques the writer has used to make his account entertaining.

Marks

1. Look at the description of the writer's encounter with the beggar (lines 1–16).

   (a) Show how the writer presents a contrast between himself and the beggar, in which the beggar appears much more secure and confident. 4

   (b) Considering their positions in society, why is this contrast comical? 1

   (c) Briefly mention another example from the passage where the writer makes himself ridiculous by coming off worst in an encounter. 1

2. Read lines 17–21. 'The thing is . . . kilos of blankets.'

   Pick an example of hyperbole from these lines and describe its effect. 2

3. A pun is a play on two meanings of the same word. Explain the pun on the word 'chips' in line 46. 2

4. A common feature of humorous writing is where a writer presents a ridiculous episode as if it is true. Pick out an example of this from the passage and explain how much truth you feel there is in the story, and how much of it is invention. 2

Total marks (12)

♦ Discuss:

   Which of these techniques do you find most effective in creating humour? Can you find any other ways in which the writer presents his topic in a humorous way?

4. ENGLISH SPOKEN HERE — AND THERE AND EVERYWHERE

In this article, Gavin Esler argues that the greatest benefit of many which the Scots have gained from their close association with England is the English language itself.

So, what have the English ever done for us? Well, nothing obviously. Except enabling ambitious Scots to make vast amounts of money running the most successful empire in history from Barbados to Ottawa to Hong Kong.

5 Okay, yes, but apart from that, what have the English ever done for us? Well, there is all that stuff about spending proportionately more of our common tax money on health care in Scotland than in England. Then there's the bit about over-representation, about more Scottish MPs at Westminster than there should be. Oh yes, and then there's the British armed forces, which remain among the strongest in the world. Plus, obviously, the fact that Scots run the
10 key ministries in London.

Yes, yes, yes! But apart from all that, what have the English ever done for us? Well, how about the language we speak? When you think about Scotland's perpetually tortured links with England perhaps the greatest and most extraordinary link is the one we think least about, the English language itself.

15 Scotland, to our great advantage, has truly been colonised by the most supple language on earth, the mother tongue of Irvine Welsh, Dylan Thomas, Seamus Heaney and George Orwell, and now, increasingly, the mother tongue of the world.

On a beach in Greece recently I heard a Norwegian woman ask the scuba-
20 diving instructor where he was from. Sweden, he said. How about you? They giggled at the fact that there they were, two Scandinavians on a Greek beach, communicating in English — of course.

Or there were the German tourists who asked the Greek waiter to bring some wine. In English, obviously. Or there was a peculiar incident I witnessed in

25   Oman when an English linguist friend tried to order a meal in Arabic. Please, the waiter, replied, I don't understand Arabic very well. I am from Pakistan. Can we speak English?

      The *International Herald Tribune* — published in Paris, but in English — reports with delicious irony that English has become the lingua franca of
30   Europe. It is now English *über alles*. To the irritation of the French and Germans, Europeans increasingly see English as the language of business, the internet and international culture. According to the French language pressure group, Le Droit de Comprendre, there are this year more signs on the streets of Paris in English than there were signs in German during the
35   Nazi occupation.

      Internal communications in any truly global company, even ones with strong European roots such as Siemens, are in English. Advertisements for jobs within multinational companies frequently specify fluency in English. Other languages are an asset, but not usually mandatory.

40   A few years ago I was filming a documentary in northern China. A young Chinese man struck up a conversation. He said he listened to the BBC World Service and also *Voice of America* on the radio, partly to hear the news, but mostly to improve his English. This, he said, was the best way to get a job with a foreign company and make serious money.

45   There is even a park in central Beijing where on a Sunday you can go to meet hundreds of ambitious Chinese students who gather to chat among themselves and to foreigners — in English. Can you imagine a similar sight in Britain? Hundreds of students assembling in the Meadows or Glasgow Green or Hyde Park or Belfast City Hall to improve their French? Of course, the
50   empire of the English language is not a complete success. On Hainan island, in southern China, another young man approached me in a restaurant and offered to help our film crew with our work. I am a transistor, the man said. I had no idea what he meant. I transist, he explained, between Chinese and English. I politely informed him that there were differences between being
55   a translator and being a transistor, and he thanked me for correcting his grammar.

But maybe, as with the Empire, Britain has given its language to the world and now lost control of it to America. British government ministers talk of double whammys, trucks not lorries, rocks instead of stones. Younger Britons sometimes pronounce schedule as skedule instead of shedule.

60

So what have the English ever done for us? Well, they have given us the world's dominant language. English. American English.

© Gavin Esler

QUESTIONS

1. Read lines 1–14. 'So what have the English . . . itself.'

   (a) 'So, what have the English ever done for us?' (line 1)

   Make clear what the **tone** of these words suggests about the attitude of the writer towards the English.

   2   A

   (b) From lines 1–10, explain in your own words **one** advantage the Scots have gained from being linked with England.

   2   U

   (c) The style of the first three paragraphs is based on a piece of dialogue from the film *Life of Brian*. Quote **two** expressions which seem to you typical of **spoken** English.

   2   A

2. *(a)* The word 'supple' (line 15) is usually applied to the body, and means strong and flexible. Explain what you think the author means by a language being 'supple'.

   1   U

   (b) In lines 16–17, the author lists four English language writers, each of whom comes from a different country within the United Kingdom. Explain how this helps reinforce his point about English being a 'supple' language.

   2   A

3. In lines 17–18 the author claims English is 'the mother tongue of the world.' Referring to any **one** of the incidents described in lines 19–27, show how the anecdote helps prove this statement true.

   2   A

4. Read lines 28–35. 'The International Herald Tribune . . . occupation.'

   (a) What is revealed about the attitude of the French and Germans to the dominance of the English language in Europe?

   1   U

   (b) The number of signs in English on the streets of Paris is compared to the number of signs seen there in German during the Nazi occupation. Explain how this comparison helps emphasise the large number of English signs.

   1   A

5. Explain how the context helps you to arrive at the meaning of 'mandatory' (line 39).

   2   U

6. Read lines 40–44. 'A few years ago . . . money.'

    In your own words, explain the advantages a Chinese person would hope to gain from being fluent in English.   2   U

7. Look at the opening sentence of the tenth paragraph 'There is even . . . English' (lines 45–47).

    Which word in this sentence emphasises how strange it is that Chinese people gather in a park to practise speaking English?   1   A

8. Look at the next two sentences 'Can you imagine . . . to improve their French?' (lines 47–49).

    Identify and explain **two** further techniques the author uses in this section to demonstrate the strangeness of the Chinese practising English in the park.   2   A

9. Show how the sentence 'But maybe . . . lost control of it to America' (lines 57–58) acts as a link in the argument at this point.   2   A

10. Show how the author uses sentence structure in the last paragraph (lines 61–62) to create a satisfactory conclusion.   2   E

11. Looking at the article as a whole, show how the author has presented the topic effectively by his use of two of the following :

    colloquial English;
    tone;
    examples;
    personal involvement;
    a 'twist' at the end.   6   E

Total marks   (30)

FOCUS ON TONE

The following questions look at how the writer varies his tone effectively.

Marks

1. The writer opens the article with a question to which he immediately gives an answer: 'Well nothing, obviously.'

   (a) Which word best describes the tone of this answer: ironic; sad; humorous; severe? 1

   (b) Explain how the sentence immediately following the answer reinforces this tone. Comment on at least **one** of the following expressions: 'except'; 'vast amounts of money'; 'the most successful empire in history'; 'from Barbados to Ottawa to Hong Kong.' 2

2. The same pattern of question / answer / development is used in paragraph two.

   (a) What does the tone of expressions like 'all that stuff' and 'the bit about' suggest about the writer's opinion of the English? 1

   (b) What do you think is the writer's actual opinion of the ways in which Scotland has been affected? 1

3. In lines 2–3 and 9 the writer uses superlatives: 'most successful'; 'strongest'.

   (a) Pick out **two** more examples of this from lines 11–14 and from lines 15–18. 2

   (b) Which **two** of the following words best describe the tone created by such superlatives: objective; neutral; positive; ironic; grudging; admiring. 2

4. Throughout the article the writer has described the benefits of the English language to the world. Describe the tone of the last phrase 'American English' and explain how it affects the rest of the article. 3

Total marks (12)

PART THREE:

TEXTUAL ANALYSIS

In the final examination you may be presented with an unseen poem with questions on it. That means, of course, that you can't prepare your answers in advance. However, you can practise looking at other poems so that you will be aware of the kind of things that are likely to be asked.

What is a poem, anyway?

Some people might say that a poem has to rhyme, or fall into regular verse divisions. Many twentieth century writers rejected that idea altogether — but their writings are still called poems.

What other qualities does a collection of words have to have before it can be described as 'poetry'?

There are endless answers to that question. Here are some people's definitions of poetry:

A good poem . . . helps to extend everyone's knowledge
of himself and the world around him.

> *(Dylan Thomas, poet, 1914–1953)*

What oft was thought, but ne'er so well
expressed.

> *(Alexander Pope, poet, 1688–1744)*

The best words in the best order.

> *(Samuel Taylor Coleridge, poet, 1772–1834)*

Peotry is sissy stuff that rhymes.

> *(Geoffrey Willans and Ronald Searle in*
> *'Down with Skool!')*

For discussion (1):

Look at the following two passages, both of which deal with the subject of an unborn child within the womb. One is written in the form of a poem while the other is in prose (which simply means any kind of writing which is not poetry).

From **You're** by Sylvia Plath

> Clownlike, happiest on your hands,
> Feet to the stars, and moon-skulled,
> Gilled like a fish . . .
> Wrapped up in yourself like a spool.
> Trawling your dark as owls do.
> Mute as a turnip from the Fourth
> Of July to All Fool's Day,
> O high-riser, my little loaf . . .
> Snug as a bud and at home
> Like a sprat in a pickle jug
> A creel of eels, all ripples.
> Jumpy as a Mexican bean.

From **The Human Body** by Anthony Smith (BBC Books, 1998)

> Only in the last eight weeks or so, when it has become too big to move around freely, does the baby spend all of its time curled up. By the ninth week, when only the size of a grape, the foetus has begun moving its muscles. By twelve weeks it has become a little acrobat, rolling from back to front, somersaulting through the amniotic fluid and waving its limbs as if to explore its surroundings.

♦ What similarities are there in these two extracts?

♦ How do they differ?

♦ What effects does the poet achieve which are not attempted in the prose passage?

For discussion (2):

Here are four more extracts from well-known poems.

♦ Do you notice anything special about the way these are written?

♦ Do they aim at any particular effect?

> O wild West Wind, thou breath of Autumn's being,
> Thou, from whose unseen presence the leaves dead
> Are driven like ghosts from an enchanter fleeing.

(Shelley: *Ode to the West Wind*)

> The ice was here, the ice was there,
> The ice was all around:
> It cracked and growled, and roared and howled . . .

(Coleridge: *The Ancient Mariner*)

> Every branch big with it,
> Bent every twig with it;
> Every fork like a white web-foot;
> Every street and pavement mute.

(Hardy: *Snow in the Suburbs*)

> Well now, look at our villa, stuck like the horn of a bull
> Just on a mountain's edge as bare as the creature's skull.

(Browning: *Up at a Villa — Down in the City*)

These discussions may have brought you closer to working out your own answer to the question raised earlier:

What is a poem?

No one simple answer to that question is possible, but in general it would be true to say that most poems would have at least these three features:

1. Economical use of language

It has been said that poetry is the art of condensing thoughts whereas prose is the art of expanding them.

In prose — whether factual writing or fiction — the writer can elaborate in as much detail as he or she wants. The writer may decide, for example, to devote several pages to describing the setting of a story.

A poet is likely to use word choice which suggests or implies more meaning than is actually stated, leaving the reader to think out these meanings for himself.

This is often done through the use of special language techniques — often called **figures of speech**. Some of these have already been looked at in Part One: Close Reading.

Checklist of figures of speech

Can you explain what the following are?

✔ Simile

✔ Metaphor

✔ Personification

✔ Alliteration

✔ Assonance

✔ Onomatopoeia

[Look back at pages 42 to 44 to find out any you have forgotten].

EXAMPLE

Here is another extract from Coleridge's poem 'The Ancient Mariner'. After being stuck in the ice, the ship begins to make progress on its journey.

> The fair breeze blew, the white foam flew,
> The furrow followed free.

Here the poet uses a combination of alliteration and onomatopoeia to emphasise how the ship is cutting through the waves in a smooth, fast, uninterrupted way. The effect of speedy progress is reinforced by the use of rhyme (blew / flew).

This is the kind of detailed commentary you should be aiming for.

Notice that the explanation of the effects always takes much longer than the lines of poetry themselves: poetry *condenses* meaning into carefully chosen words.

♦ The extract from Sylvia Plath's poem 'You're' on page 85 is full of similes and metaphors which compare the unborn child to many different subjects.

Make a list of these — there are at least eleven of them.
Then decide which ones are similes and which are metaphors.

Next, try to think what the comparison tells us about the baby.

You could write out your answers in the form of a table like the one below. One example has been done for you.

EXAMPLE	FIGURE OF SPEECH	WHAT THE BABY IS COMPARED TO	WHAT THIS TELLS US ABOUT THE BABY
'a creel of eels'	metaphor	The baby is compared to a basket containing eels.	The baby is constantly wriggling its arms and legs within the confined space of the womb.

2. *Expression of feelings*

Poems are rarely about making points or conveying information. Most concentrate on expressing the poet's thoughts and feelings.

In many of the best poems we feel that we share the feelings described but could not have put these feelings into words as convincingly.

♦ In this first world war poem by Siegfried Sassoon, the poet describes the contrast between the feelings of the mother whose son has died and those of the officer who brings her the news.

Make a list of the feelings and emotions you notice here (anger, pride, love, etc.), then write down the words and phrases used to convey these feelings.

The Hero

'Jack fell as he'd have wished', the Mother said.
And folded up the letter that she'd read.
'The Colonel writes so nicely.' Something broke
In the tired voice that quavered to a choke.
She half looked up. 'We mothers are so proud
Of our dead soldiers.' Then her face was bowed.

Quietly, the Brother Officer went out.
He'd told the poor old dear some gallant lies
That she would nourish all her days, no doubt.
For while he coughed and mumbled, her weak eyes
Had shone with gentle triumph, brimmed with joy,
Because he'd been so brave, her glorious boy.

He thought how 'Jack', cold-footed, useless swine,
Had panicked down the trench that night the mine
Went up at Wicked Corner; how he'd tried
To get sent home, and how, at last, he died,
Blown to small bits. And no one seemed to care
Except that lonely woman with white hair.

© Siegfried Sassoon

3. **Element of Pattern**

Some people feel that a poem has to fall into regular verses and must rhyme. This kind of poem is often satisfying as it has a rhythm and pace to it which makes it easier to remember.

> There lived a wife at Usher's well,
> And a wealthy wife was she;
> She had three stout and stalwart sons,
> And sent them o'er the sea.

This verse follows a typical four line verse form with a rhyme scheme of *a b c b*.

During the twentieth century many poets chose to write in what became known as 'free verse' — free, that is, from restrictions of verse form or rhyming pattern. However, use of deliberately short or long lines, repetition, etc., can still give free verse some kind of pattern or structure.

♦   What do you notice about the pattern and structure of these extracts from three well-known poems?

> Alone, alone, all, all alone,
> Alone on a wide, wide sea!
> And never a saint took pity on
> My soul in agony.

(from Coleridge's The Ancient Mariner)

> Four grey walls, and four grey towers,
> Overlook a space of flowers,
> And the silent isle imbowers
> The Lady of Shalott.

(from Tennyson's The Lady of Shallot)

> And where the water had dripped from the tap, in a small clearness,
> He sipped with his straight mouth,
> Softly drank through his straight gums into his slack long body
>   Silently.

(from Snake by D. H. Lawrence)

PART FOUR:

PRACTICE
in
TEXTUAL ANALYSIS

The Competition

This poem was written by a modern Scottish poet, Douglas Dunn.

When I was ten, going to Hamilton
On the Leyland bus named for Eddlewood,
A boy with an aeroplane just like mine
Zoomed at his war games in the seat in front.
5 I'd never seen such a school uniform —
As brown as the manure in Cousar's coup   *coup: a place for emptying*
Where someone's city cousin had jumped in   *rubbish*
Having been told it was 'just sand' —
One of Glasgow's best fee-paying places,
10 Brown as barrowloads from the blue-bottled byre.
I couldn't help it; I had to talk to him
And tell him I, too, had a Hurricane.
His mother pulled him to her; he sat sullen,   *sullen: silent, sulky*
As if I'd spoiled his game. I spoke again,
15 And he called me a poor boy, who should shut up.
I'd never thought of it like that.
The summer tenements were so dry I cried.
My grandfather wouldn't give *him* sixpence;
He'd never have a grudge as lovely as mine.

20 Years later, running in a race, barefooted
As I'd trained my spikes to ruin, convinced
My best competitor was him, I ran into
The worst weathers of pain, determined to win,
But on the last lap, inches from the tape, was beaten
25 By someone from Shotts Miners' Welfare Harriers Club.   *Harrier:*
a cross-country runner

© Douglas Dunn

The setting of the poem

Douglas Dunn is one of the most successful of modern Scottish poets. He was born in Inchinnan, Renfrewshire, in 1942 and worked as a librarian before becoming a full time writer.

Douglas Dunn has said that: *My writing is concerned with my background and my past*.

♦ Write down details from the poem which help to locate the incident in real place and at a particular time.

The theme of the poem

The poem is about how the boy gradually becomes aware of social differences. To the mother and boy on the bus he is 'a poor boy', but Dunn had 'never thought of it like that'.

♦ What are Douglas Dunn's feelings towards each of the following people?

Character	Feeling	Evidence
Boy on the bus		
The city cousin		
Boy's mother		
Dunn's grandfather		
The athlete		

If the poem had stopped at the end of verse one, the message might have been a straightforward one about snobbery and social class differences.

But there is more to it than that.

As he grows up Dunn remembers the incident and derives a kind of satisfaction from thinking he had been the victim of social injustice, as shown by the line

He'd never have a grudge as lovely as mine.

Years later, Dunn imagines he has his chance to get even by beating this boy in a race. In the end, however, the runner turns out to be *someone from Shotts Miners' Welfare Harrier Club* — in other words, somebody from a similar background to his own.

♦   What point do you think Douglas Dunn is making here?

The style of the poem

Textual analysis of poetry is not just about ideas but about the methods used by poets to put their ideas across. If, as Coleridge said, poetry is *the best words in the best orde*r, we need to consider why the poet chooses particular words and why he orders, or structures, them in a certain way.

'The best words'

Poets often try to create an impression of a subject by comparing it with something that the reader might be familiar with. This technique is called **imagery** and involves figures of speech such as **simile**, **metaphor** and **personification**.

♦   *What figures of speech are used in the following examples? What kind of picture do these lines bring into your mind?*

Zoomed at his war games in the seat in front.

As brown as the manure in Cousar's coup.

Brown as barrowloads from the blue-bottled byre.

'The best order'

The arrangement of ideas in a poem can often be affected by the punctuation and sentence structure. (Look back at page 19 to remind yourself of terms such as **list, repetition** and **climax**. The punctuation terms on page 22 — **commas, colons, semi-colons, inverted commas,** and **dashes for parenthesis** are just as relevant to poetry questions).

♦   *How many of these techniques can you find in Douglas Dunn's poem?*

Child with Pillar Box and Bin Bags

This poem was written by Kathleen Jamie, another modern Scottish poet. She describes it as an 'inner-city poem' which is concerned with 'love', 'poverty' and 'freedom of choice'.

♦ *Read the poem and answer the questions which follow.*
These are laid out in the textual analysis format.

But it was the shadowed street-side she chose
While Victor Gold the bookies basked
In conquered sunlight, and though
Dalry Road Licensed Grocer gloried and cast
5   Fascinating shadows she chose
The side dark in the shade of tenements;
That corner where Universal Stores' (closed
For modernisation), blank hoarding blocked
Her view as if that process were illegal;
10   She chose to photograph her baby here,
The corner with the pillar box.
In his buggy, which she swung to face her.
She took four steps back, but
The baby in his buggy rolled toward the kerb.

15   She crossed the ground in no time.
It was fearful as Niagara,
She ran to put the brake on, and returned
to lift the camera, a cheap one.
The tenements of Caledonian Place neither
20   Watched nor looked away; they are friendly buildings.
The traffic ground, the buildings shook, the baby breathed
And maybe gurgled at his mother as she
Smiled to make him smile in his picture;
Which she took on the kerb in the shadowed corner,
25   Beside the post-box, under tenements, before the
Bin bags hot in the sun that shone
On them, on dogs, on people on the other side
The other side of the street to that she'd chosen,
If she'd chosen or thought it possible to choose.

© Kathleen Jamie

QUESTIONS

Marks

1. Describe the incident that this poem deals with. 2

2. *(a)* What was it that the poet found surprising? 2

   (b) How is this reinforced by the sentence structure used in the opening line? 2

3. The poet spends time describing the area where the incident took place.

   (a) Pick out four different details of the surroundings which she mentions. 4

   (b) Choose two of these and comment on what they add to the atmosphere of the poem. 2

4. Much of the description in the poem is concerned with the contrast of light and shade. Quote an example of this contrast and comment on any aspect of the word choice used. 4

5. The technique of alliteration is used several times in this poem.

   (a) Quote an example of this. 1

   (b) Comment on the effect the poet is aiming at. 2

6. *(a)* What happens in lines 14–18? 2

   (b) Comment on any aspect of the poet's use of language to convey a sense of danger in these lines. 3

7. What point do you think the poet is making in the final four lines? 3

8. Talking about this poem, the poet, Kathleen Jamie, said: 'That listing, piling way of writing, with many concealed and half-rhymes, I find suspiciously quick and easy.'

   Find examples of this feature of her writing from anywhere in the poem and comment on whether you think it is effective. 3

   Total marks (30)

Unlucky Boat

The poet George Mackay Brown lived most of his life in Orkney and wrote about the Orkney people, their way of life, customs and beliefs.

That boat has killed three people. Building her
Sib drove a nail through his thumb. He died in his croft
Bunged to the eyes with rust and penicillin.
One evening when the Flow was a bar of silver
5 Under the moon, and Mansie and Tom with wands
Were putting a spell on cuithes*, she dipped a bow
And ushered Mansie, his pipe still in his teeth,
To meet the cold green angels. They hauled her up
Among the rocks, right in the path of Angus,
10 Whose neck, rigid with pints from the Dounby Market,
Snapped like a barley stalk . . . There she lies,
A leprous unlucky bitch, in the quarry of Moan.

Tinkers, going past, make the sign of the cross.

© George Mackay Brown

* a type of fish

QUESTIONS

Marks

1. Comment on the effectiveness of the first sentence as an opening to the poem.

2

2, Without using quotations, summarise how each of the three men died.

6

3. What is there in the poem to suggest the people are superstitious?

2

4. Boats are commonly referred to as 'she' rather than 'it'. How does the poet develop this use of personification throughout the entire poem?

4

5. How is the sudden nature of Mansie's death conveyed?

2

6. Why do you think the angels are described as 'cold' and 'green'?

2

7. To what extent does the poem convince you that the deaths of the men were caused entirely by the boat?

4

8. The language of the poem is a mixture of poetic description and imagery on the one hand and simple, colloquial language on the other. Find an example of each type of language and comment on the effectiveness of each.

4

9. One critic has written that 'George Mackay Brown looks at people involved with the elements. In the settled Orkney communities, men and women . . . gain hard-earned livelihoods between fertile fields and the sea where tragedy is never far away. The poet shares many of the experiences of the people about whom he writes.'

How far do you feel that these comments apply to 'Unlucky Boat'?

4

Total marks (30)

The Love Song of J. Alfred Prufrock (lines 1–22)

In this extract from a poem by T.S. Eliot, a person who feels rather insecure about himself is going through an area of a town on his way somewhere. The reader needs to think about his destination and who he is with, what his purpose is and so on, as these points are not fully explained.

Let us go then, you and I,
When the evening is spread out against the sky
Like a patient etherised* upon a table;
Let us go, through certain half-deserted streets,
5   The muttering retreats
Of restless nights in one-night cheap hotels
And sawdust restaurants with oyster-shells:
Streets that follow like a tedious argument
Of insidious intent
10   To lead you to an overwhelming question . . .
Oh, do not ask, 'What is it?'
Let us go and make our visit.

In the room the women come and go
Talking of Michelangelo.**

15   The yellow fog that rubs its back upon the window-panes,
The yellow smoke that rubs its muzzle on the window-panes
Licked its tongue into the corners of the evening,
Lingered upon the pools that stand in drains,
Let fall upon its back the soot that falls from chimneys,
20   Slipped by the terrace, made a sudden leap,
And seeing that it was a soft October night,
Curled once about the house, and fell asleep.

© T.S. Eliot

---

*   Ether: a substance used in medicine as an anaesthetic.

**   Michelangelo: famous painter and sculptor of the Italian Renaissance period.

QUESTIONS

Marks

1. What is the comparison suggested in lines 2–3?

   2

2. What are the implications of this for the mood of the rest of the poem?

   2

3. *(a)* What kind of area do the characters walk through?

   2

   (b) Select two descriptive details from lines 4–7 and comment on how they add to your impression of the area.

   4

4. What might the 'overwhelming question' be (line 10)?

   2

5. Consider the effect of any aspect of sentence structure, sentence length and punctuation in lines 1–12.

   3

6. How has the setting changed in lines 13–14?

   2

7. Why might the women be talking of Michelangelo?

   2

8. *(a)* Comment in detail on the comparison used in lines 15–22.

   3

   (b) What kind of atmosphere is created in these lines? Comment in detail on the poet's word choice.

   3

9. What connections might there be between the three sections of the poem?

   3

10. Whom do you imagine is the narrator in this poem? Is there any point at which the narrative point of view changes?

    2

Total marks (30)

YOUR NOTES

ACKNOWLEDGEMENTS

We hereby acknowledge the use of copyright material in this book
and are grateful to those for granting this permission.

Extract from *Fever Pitch*
by Nick Hornby.
(Victor Gollancz, 1992) © Nick Hornby, 1992.
Reprinted by permission of the publisher Penguin UK.

Extract from *ART A Crash Course*
by Julian Freeman.
© The Ivy Press Limited, 1998.
Reprinted by permission of the publisher Simon & Schuster.

Kidspoem / Bairnsang
by the playwright Liz Lochhead.
Reprinted by permission of The Rod Hall Agency Limited as the playwright's agent.

Extract from *DR NO*
by Ian Fleming.
Reproduced with the permission of Ian Fleming (Glidrose) Publications Ltd.
DR NO by Ian Fleming copyright © Glidrose Productions Ltd, 1958.

Extract from *The Lost Continent*
by Bill Bryson.
© Bill Bryson 1989. Extracted from *The Lost Continent*,
published by Black Swan, a division of Transworld Publishers.
All rights reserved.

Watery Grave Robbers
by Jeremy Hodges.
From an article in the *Scottish Daily Mail*.

The mixed blessing of eternal life
by Collette Douglas Home.
Reprinted by permission of the *Daily Mail*.

'It's a Scottish thing — that even beggars have chips on their shoulders'
TUESDAY with David Gray.
Article from *The Scotsman* (Features) June 1999.

English spoken here — and there and everywhere
This article by Gavin Esler, writer and broadcaster,
appeared in his weekly column in *The Scotsman*.

ACKNOWLEDGEMENTS (cont'd)

Extract from *You're*
from *COLLECTED POEMS*
by Sylvia Plath.
Reprinted by permission of the publisher Faber and Faber Ltd.

The Hero
by Siegfried Sassoon.
Copyright Siegfried Sassoon reprinted by kind permission of George Sassoon.

The Competition
from *SELECTED POEMS*
by Douglas Dunn.
Reprinted by permission of the publisher Faber and Faber Ltd.

Child with Pillar Box and Bin Bags
© Kathleen Jamie.
Reprinted by permission of the author Kathleen Jamie.

Unlucky Boat from *TRAVELLERS*
by George Mackay Brown.
Reprinted by permission of the publisher John Murray (Publishers) Ltd.

Extract from *The Love Song of J. Alfred Prufrock*
from *COLLECTED POEMS 1909–1962*
by T.S. Eliot.
Reprinted by permission of the publisher Faber and Faber Ltd.